STUDY GUIDE
TO ACCOMPANY

MW00575462

THE RESTAURANT
From Concept to Operation

SEVENTH EDITION

JOHN R. WALKER, D.B.A., C.H.A., F.M.P.
CONTRIBUTING AUTHOR TINA POWERS

WILEY

This book is printed on acid-free paper. ∞

Published by John Wiley and Sons, Inc., Hoboken, New Jersey.
Published simultaneously in Canada.

For general information on our other products and services, or technical support, please contact our Customer Care Department within the United States at 800-762-2974, outside the United States at 317-572-3993 or fax 317-572-4002.

Wiley also publishes its books in a variety of electronic formats. Some content that appears in print may not be available in electronic books.

For more information about Wiley products, visit our Web site at www.wiley.com.

Library of Congress Cataloging-in-Publication Data:

ISBN: 978-1-118-62960-4

Printed in the United States of America

10   9   8   7   6   5   4   3   2   1

TABLE OF CONTENTS

TO THE STUDENT

This *Study Guide* is a student companion to *The Restaurant: From Concept to Operation, Seventh Edition.* It serves as a resource to help you study and review the material in the text. This supplement is arranged by chapter corresponding to the 15 chapters in *Seventh Edition.* Tina Powers has helped to prepare the features within this supplement to ensure that each chapter includes several resources to help you review the material and exercises that you can use to test your own knowledge of the key topics and concepts. These resources include the following:

Introduction
A brief opening description to the chapter that outlines the overall theme and approach to the topics covered.

Objectives
These highlight the key concepts presented in the chapter and provide a road map of the specific knowledge and skills you should be learning from reading the chapter.

Chapter Outline
Provides a detailed summary of the key points presented in the chapter.

True or False Questions
True or False questions are provided for each chapter. These questions test your understanding of key terms and concepts.

Fill in the Blanks: Key Term Review
Key Term Review questions ask you to fill in the blanks with the appropriate term or phrase to complete the sentence and help to reinforce your comprehension of the concepts presented in the chapter.

Multiple Choice Questions: Concept Review
Multiple Choice Questions ask you to choose the most appropriate response to each question. These questions ensure that you fully comprehend the key concepts covered in each chapter.

Short Answer Questions
Thought-provoking questions based upon the material presented in the chapter test the knowledge you have gained from studying the chapter.

Internet Exercise
Surf the Web for answers to various questions.

Activity
Suggested activities that enable students to exercise the specific knowledge and skills learned from reading the chapter. These activities offer the opportunity for students to observably carry out the learning objectives presented at the beginning of the chapter—from concept to operation.

CHAPTER 1:
INTRODUCTION

INTRODUCTION

Restaurants play a significant role in our lifestyles, and dining out is a popular social activity. Everyone needs to eat—so, to enjoy good food and perhaps wine in the company of friends and in pleasant surroundings is one of life's pleasures. Eating out has become a way of life for families. Today, more meals than ever are being eaten away from home. This chapter outlines the history of restaurants. In addition, various aspects of opening restaurants are reviewed.

OBJECTIVES

After reading and studying this chapter, you should be able to:
- o Discuss reasons why some people open restaurants
- o List some challenges of restaurant operation
- o Outline the history of restaurants
- o Compare the advantages and disadvantages of buying, building, and franchising restaurants

CHAPTER OUTLINE

Introduction
- o Restaurants play a significant role in our lifestyles
    - o Dining out is a social activity
    - o Successful restaurants offer a reasonable return on investment
    - o Restaurant concept determines talents required
    - o No substitute for experience
- o Reason for going into the restaurant business
    - o Money
    - o Potential for buyout
    - o Place to socialize
    - o Changing work environment
    - o Challenge
    - o Habit
    - o Fun lifestyle
    - o Too much time on your hands
    - o Opportunity to express yourself

Early History of Eating Out
- o Long history
  - o 1700 B.C.E. taverns
  - o 512 B.C.E. Ancient Egypt public dining place
  - o 70 A.D. Herculaneum, Rome
  - o 1200 London cooking houses
  - o 1550 Constantinople café
  - o 1650 Oxford coffee house

French Culinary History
- o Public dining room-First restaurant
- o 1767: Boulanger-sold soup as a *restorantes* or restorative
- o 1782: Beauvilliers- First restaurant Grand Tavern de Londres
- o 1794: French Revolution
  - o Chefs to the former nobility suddenly had no employment Some stayed and opened restaurants, some went to Europe; many fled to America

Birth of Restaurants in America
- o 1634: Coles Ordinary, Boston Massachusetts
- o 1783: John Adams Tavern
- o 1826: Union Oyster House, Boston Massachusetts

Delmonico's
- o 1832-1900: New York City
  - o 1832: Delmonico's
  - o 1848: Sweeney's
  - o 1888: Katz' Deli

American Style Restaurants
- o 1919: 42,600 restaurants in America
  - o Continued expansion

Reponses to Changing Times
- o 1921: White Castle-First hamburger chain
- o 1927: Drive-ins, root beer and ice cream stands
- o 1929: Great Depression rebound-Rainbow Room, Trader Vic's
- o WWII Influence
  - o Americans took to the road
  - o Rapid development of hotels and coffee shops

Fast Food Restaurants
- o Kentucky Fried Chicken, "Colonel" Harland Sanders
- o McDonald's, Ray Kroc
  - o 1960s and 1970s:
  - o Emergence of chains (e.g., Taco Bell)

Challenges of Restaurant Operation

- o Include
    - o Long hours; fatigue and burn out.
    - o Little job security for managers working for others
    - o Possibility of losing investments and investors
    - o Consumers careful how they spend their money
- o Restaurant operators and staff must
    - o Enjoy serving people
    - o Handle frustration easily
    - o Be tireless and outgoing
    - o Have lots of energy and stamina
    - o Be able to withstand pressure
    - o Have knowledge of food (highly desirable)
- o Starting a restaurant involves high risk
    - o Must be taken to achieve success
- o Results of Dr. Parsa's study
    - o Three year period Failure rate: 59%
    - o Many fail due to personal reasons involving the owner or owners
    - o While family owned restaurants survive the start-up period, many restaurants fail because of family problems. Too many hours too much energy, no energy left for balanced family life.
    - o When husband and wife operate a restaurant as a team, both must enjoy the business and be highly motivated to make it successful.

Buy, Build, Franchise or Manage
- o Several career and investment options
    - o Buy an existing restaurant, operate it as is, or change its concept
    - o Build a new restaurant and operate it
    - o Purchase a franchise and operate the franchise restaurant
    - o Manage a restaurant for someone else either as Individual or a chain

Comparing the advantage and disadvantages of buying, building, franchise or working as a professional manager.
- o Individuals should assess:
    - o Temperament
    - o Ambition
    - o Ability to cope with frustrations
    - o Different risks and potential rewards
    - o Aesthetic personal desire

Successful existing restaurants can be analyzed
- o Borrow good points and practices
    - o Modify and improve if possible
- o Successful mix
    - o One that is better than the competition

Starting from Scratch

- o Would be restaurant operators
    - o Mix of different experiences in the business
- o Industry does not have enough employees
    - o Turnover rate is high
- o Business is highly competitive
    - o Requires inordinate energy, long hours, and willingness to accept a low salary
    - o Students seek jobs in name restaurants or go abroad building their skills and rounding out resumes.

Restaurants as Roads to Riches
- o Most common reason people seek restaurant ownership
    - o Possible financial rewards
- o Economic troubles
    - o Lead to bankruptcy filings (e.g., Bennigan's and Starbucks)
        - o Costs are up
        - o Sales are down
- o This book will help you with
    - o Ownership
    - o Development of a business plan
    - o Marketing/Sales
    - o Location
    - o Who's on your team?
    - o Design/Ambiance
    - o Menu
    - o Beverages
    - o Legal
    - o Budgets
    - o Control
    - o Service
    - o Management
    - o Operations

Global Issues
- o Many of the world's top restaurants have similar concerns and overall goals
    - o Innovative menu concepts
    - o Successful marketing
    - o Site selection
    - o Remodeling/capital investments
- o Creating a unique menu/supports overall theme
    - o Using more focused forms of promotion/social media
- o Technology has shrunk the playing field
- o Optimizing investments in remodeling and capital expenditures is the goal

TRUE OR FALSE QUESTIONS

On the following questions, answer whether the statement provided is true or false.

T (F) 1. Union Oyster House, located in ~~Cambridge~~ Boston, Massachusetts, is thought to be one of the first restaurants in America.

(T) F 2. The first restaurant ever was called a "public dining room" and originated in France.

T (F) 3. When opening a restaurant, one should never "borrow" ideas from existing restaurants.

T (F) 4. Franchising and managing involve the least financial risk in that the restaurant format.

T (F) 5. The restaurant industry currently has an overflow of employees. *Turnover* ↑

(T) F 6. A 100-seat restaurant, fully equipped, costs anywhere from $6,000 to $10,000 or more per seat.

(T) F 7. The French Revolution in 1794 literally caused heads to roll, causing many chefs (to the former nobility) to become unemployed.

(T) F 8. A sandwich shop can usually be opened for less than $30,000.

T (F) 9. The biggest reason thousands of people seek restaurant ownership is the possible psychological rewards.

(T) (F) 10. Technology has expanded the playing field.

(T) (F) 11. Howard Johnson is credited with being the first restaurant to franchise.

(T) F 12. The successful restaurateur will have a menu that also supports their overall theme.

FILL IN THE BLANKS: KEY TERM REVIEW

On the following questions, fill in the blank with the most appropriate key term.

1. The kind of restaurant __concept__ you select determines to a large extent the talents that will be required of employees.

2. A(n) __Franchise__ includes building design, menu, and marketing plans, which already have been tested in the marketplace.

3. All managers should carry thermometers in their shirt pockets so they can check at any time that food is served at exactly the correct temperature. This is an example of __quality control__.

4. The term __restaurant__ came to the United States in 1794 via a French refugee from the guillotine.

5. According to the __NRA__ the restaurant industry totals $566 billion in sales.

MULTIPLE CHOICE QUESTIONS: CONCEPT REVIEW
On the following questions, circle the choice that best answers the question.

1. Which of the following individuals is thought to be the first restaurant proprietor?
    a. Parsa
    b. Boulanger
    c. Bailleul
    d. Delmonico

2. Which of the following was located in New York City and is thought to be the one of first restaurants in America?
    a. Delmonico's
    b. Julian's Tavern
    c. Grand Tavern
    d. Julien's Restaurator

3. Which of the following involves the least financial risk, yet the psychological risk may be high?
    a. building
    b. buying
    c. managing
    d. franchising

4. Which of the following requires the highest original investment?
    a. building
    b. buying
    c. managing
    d. franchising

5. A flip is made from:
    a. vodka and orange juice
    b. rum, orange juice and cranberry juice
    c. rum, beer, beaten eggs, and spices
    d. vodka and eggnog

6. In working for others, managers have:
   a. no job security
   b. little job security
   c. moderate job security
   d. a lot of job security

7. The term restaurant came to the United States via a French refugee named:
   a. Boulanger
   b. Bailleul
   c. Delmonico
   d. Paypalt

8. Probably the biggest reason thousands of people seek restaurant ownership is the:
   a. risk
   b. possible financial rewards
   c. challenge
   d. possible psychological rewards

9. A 100-seat restaurant, fully equipped, costs anywhere from:
   a. $1000 to $2000 per seat
   b. $2000 to $3000 per seat
   c. $5000 to $6000 per seat
   d. $6,000 to $10,000 or more per seat

10. The first restaurant ever was called a:
    a. public dining room
    b. private diner
    c. diner
    d. café

11. A land marked study H.G. Parsa at Ohio State University found the actual failure rate of restaurants in Columbus, Ohio was:
    a. 59% for a three-year period
    b. 19% for a three-year period
    c. 80% for a three-year period
    d. 10% for a three-year period

12. Which of the following involves the highest risks overall?
    a. building
    b. buying
    c. managing
    d. franchising

13. Declining consumer confidence took a bite out of restaurants' sales and profits in 2007-2012, leading to the closure of more than _____ Starbucks locations.
    a. 600
    b. 1000
    c. 1600
    d. 2200

14. Boulanger believed that which of the following was the cure to all sorts of illnesses?
    a. vegetables
    b. carrot juice
    c. thyme
    d. soup

15. According to the National Restaurant Association, the restaurant industry is expected to add _____ jobs by 2020.
    a. 1.3 million
    b. 200,000
    c. 2.2 million
    d. 500,000

16. What gives the restaurant the ability to target specific groups of guests that may have certain noticeable buying behaviors.
    a. radio ads
    b. social media
    c. newsprint inserts
    d. TV spots

17. A $5,000 investment in KFC in 1964 was worth how much, five years later?
    a. 1.5 million
    b. 2.5 million
    c. 3.5 million
    d. 4.5 million

18. About how many restaurants were in this country in 1919?
    a. 10,600
    b. 22,000
    c. 42,600
    d. 126,400

19. The beginning of the American restaurant industry is usually said to be in 1634, when _____ opened an establishment in Boston.
    a. Coles
    b. Parsa
    c. Boulanger
    d. Bailleul

20. The first café was established in _____ in 1550.
    a. Paris
    b. Constantinople
    c. Boston
    d. New York

21. Over _____ restaurants in New York have celebrated their 100th year birthday.
    a. 25
    b. 30
    c. 35
    d. 40

SHORT ANSWER QUESTIONS

1. How did restaurants first come to America?

2. Compare the advantages and disadvantages of **buying** a restaurant.

3. Compare the advantages and disadvantages of **building** a restaurant.

4. Compare the advantages and disadvantages of **franchising** a restaurant.

5. Compare the advantages and disadvantages of **managing** a restaurant.

6. Independent operators can develop a personal following and appeal to **what type** of customer that are bored with chain operators and menus.
7. Describe **ownership.**
8. **Who** is on your restaurant team**?**
9. What is involved in the **development of a good business plan?**
10. How is **social media** used in promoting restaurants?

INTERNET EXERCISE

1. Utilizing one of the social media sites such as Facebook, locate the webpage or blog for two restaurants: one a franchise of your choice, and the other, an independent restaurant for comparison. Find out for each one, how long they have been in business, what their restaurant concepts are, and compare their menus. Note if they have an on line ordering system, and anything else that makes them stand out or unique.

*Examples: McDonalds, Popeye's Chicken, or Taco Bell, as a franchise, and Radius, Mustards Grill, or WD 50 as an independent restaurant.

ACTIVITY

1. Would you prefer to buy, build, franchise, or manage a restaurant? Develop your own personal chart comparing the advantages and disadvantages of each as they relate to your personal life.

CHAPTER 2:
RESTAURANTS AND THEIR OWNERS

INTRODUCTION

This chapter describes the kinds and characteristics of restaurants and their owners. Restaurant categories have not been universally agreed on and, from time to time, new segments are conceived in the literature. A comparison of corporate-owned, independent, and franchised restaurants is made. Chef-owner restaurateurs, notable female restaurateurs, celebrity chefs, and centralized home delivery restaurants are also discussed.

OBJECTIVES

After reading and studying this chapter, you should be able to:
- o   List and describe the various kinds and characteristics of restaurants
- o   Compare and contrast chain, franchised, and independent restaurant operations
- o   Describe the advantages and disadvantages of chef-owned restaurants
- o   Identify several well-known celebrity chefs
- o   Define what a centralized home delivery restaurant is and what it offers

CHAPTER OUTLINE

Kinds and Characteristics of Restaurants
- o   Segments:
  - o   Chain or independent (indy) and franchise restaurants
  - o   Quick-service (QSR), sandwich
  - o   Fast casual
  - o   Family
  - o   Casual
  - o   Fine dining
  - o   Other

Chain or Independent
- o   Impression that huge quick-service chains dominate restaurant business is misleading.
  - o   Chain restaurants have some advantages and disadvantages over independent restaurants. Advantages include:
    - o   Recognition in the marketplace
    - o   Greater advertising clout
    - o   Sophisticated systems development
    - o   Discounted purchasing

- o   Independent restaurant advantages

- o Relatively easy to open
- o Restaurateur can "do their own thing"
- o Plenty of room in certain locations
- o Buy out by larger companies
- o Acquire financing for expansion

Franchised Restaurants

- o For those who lack extensive experience
- o Involves fewer risks
- o Franchisers will need to know if you:
  - o Share values, mission, ways of doing business
  - o Have been successful
  - o Possess motivation to succeed
  - o Have enough money to purchase and operate
  - o Have the ability to spend time on franchise
  - o Training from the bottom up and all areas of the operation
- o Franchising involves
  - o Building design
  - o Menu and marketing plans
  - o Marketing tested/proven concepts
  - o Training provided
  - o Marketing and management support
  - o Franchising fees, royalty fees, advertising royalty and requirements of personal net worth.
- o Franchisors will provide
  - o Help with site selection
  - o Assistance with design and building preparation
  - o Help with preparation for opening
  - o Training of managers and staff
  - o Planning and implementation of preopening marketing strategies
  - o Unit visits and ongoing operating advice

Sandwich Shops

- o Characteristics
  - o Simple to open and operate
  - o Little or no cooking required
  - o Limited kitchen equipment needed
- o Examples
  - o Jimmy John's gourmet sandwich shop
  - o The Sandwich Shop in San Francisco
  - o Subway

Quick-Service

- o 1870s: Plate House
  - o First known quick-service restaurant
- o Characteristics
  - o Many precook or partially cook food
  - o Goal is to serve maximum number of customers in a minimum amount of time
  - o Food is paid for before service
  - o Limited menus

Pop-Up Restaurants
- o Appear only for a few days, with up front price.
  - o Social media play roll in filling seats
  - o Challenges include ordering the right amount of food
    - o Health permits
    - o Competent staff
    - o Location
- o Concept started in London and quickly spread around the world.
- o People keep track via social media like Twitter or Facebook

Food Trucks
- o Next step up from sidewalk food carts
- o Elevation of the form-quality, variety and sheer numbers
  - o Competition to restaurants
  - o Enhance rather than detract from city's food culture and competition
  - o Some cities have food truck fiestas and other rallies.

Quick Casual Restaurants
- o Defining traits
  - o Use of high-quality ingredients
  - o Fresh made-to-order menu items
  - o Healthy options
  - o Limited or self-serving formats
  - o Upscale décor
  - o Carry-out meals
  - o Includes bakery-cafés

Family Restaurants
- o Characteristics
  - o Grew out of coffee shop-style restaurant
  - o Frequently located within easy reach of suburbs
  - o Informal
  - o Some offer wine and beer
  - o Most offer no alcoholic beverages
  - o Prominent chains: Bob Evans, Perkins, Marie Callender's, Cracker Barrel, and Waffle House to name a few.

Casual Restaurants

- o Characteristics
  - o Fits societal trend of a relaxed lifestyle
  - o Signature food items
  - o Creative bar menus or enhanced wine service
  - o Comfortable, homey décor
- o Examples
  - o Applebee's, Outback, Chili's, etc.

Fine-Dining Restaurants
- o Characteristics
  - o Expensive and enjoyed leisurely
  - o Very low table turnover
  - o Customers: special occasions and business
- o Restaurants are small
  - o Usually less than 100 seats
  - o Proprietor- or partner-owned
  - o Rent can be high
  - o Labor is high
  - o Profit from wine sales
  - o Appointments can be costly
  - o Menu includes expensive items such as Scottish smoked salmon, caviar and truffles.
  - o Trend setting with smaller portions

Hotel Restaurants
- o Luxury hotels can be counted on to have restaurants with well trained and experienced chefs.
- o Hotel restaurants have elegant décor, table setting service and food
- o Taverns and Inns come together was the root of full service hotels.
- o Many hotels have a three meal style restaurant and many are open late with 24 hour room service.
- o Hotel restaurants were berated in the past but have become shining stars in many hospitality operations.
- o Many hotels outsource restaurant operations.

Steakhouses
- o Characteristics
  - o Limited menu caters to a well-identified market (i.e. steak eaters)
  - o Service ranges from walk-up to high-end
  - o High food costs (as high as 50%)
  - o Low labor costs (as low as 12%)
  - o Majority of customers are men

Lore of Steak
- o Steaks vary
  - o Types include
    - o Tenderloin: most tender and runs along backbone
    - o T-bone: cut from the small end of loin
    - o Porterhouse: T-bone and tenderloin
    - o New York Strip: compact, dense, and boneless
    - o Delmonico: small, often boned steak, taken from the front section of the short loin
    - o Sirloin: comes from just in front of the round, between the rump and shank
- o High-end operations need a million people as a customer base.
  - o Considerable investments in building, fixtures and equipment
  - o Forty percent or more serve well-aged beef

Outback Steakhouse
- o Most successful concepts of all time
  - o "No rules, just right"
  - o Almost everything is made fresh daily
  - o Diversified into Italian food
- o Five principles for success:
  - o Hospitality
  - o Sharing
  - o Quality
  - o Fun
  - o Courage

Seafood Restaurants
- o Colonial America
  - o Seafood was a staple food in the taverns
- o Characteristics
  - o Many are independently operated
- o Red Lobster is the largest chain
  - o 700 restaurants
- o Farm-bred fish
  - o Changing the cost and kinds available
  - o Aquaculture is predicted to grow and may bring the price of seafood down

Ethnic Restaurants
Mexican restaurant
- o Characteristics
  - o Menu is often built around tortillas, ground beef, cilantro, chilies, rice, and beans
  - o Relatively inexpensive
  - o Labor costs are also low
  - o Menus, décor, and music are often colorful and exciting
  - o Menus may include tasty seafood items and spicy sauces
Italian Restaurants

o Characteristics
    o Largest number of U.S. ethnic restaurants
    o Offer an array of opportunities for franchisees
    o Owe their origins largely to poor immigrants from southern Italy
    o Pizza is native to Naples
    o Chain operators are spreading the pasta concept (e.g., Olive Garden)

Asian Restaurants
o Characteristics
    o Small percentage of restaurants in America
    o Historically, owned by hardworking ethnic Chinese families
    o Cooking revolves around the wok
    o China is divided into culinary districts

Theme Restaurants
o Characteristics
    o Built around emphasizing fun and fantasy
    o Comparatively short life cycle
    o Do well outside major tourist attractions
    o Costs are high
o Martin M. Pegler: *Theme Restaurant Design*
    o Theme restaurant categories

Coffee Shops
o Characteristics
    o Long part of our culture and history
    o Originally created based on Italian bars
    o Modified to include wider variety of beverages
    o Chain or independent
o Requirements
    o Good name and location, permits, coffee and espresso machine, limited kitchen equipment, tables, chairs, and some decorations

Chef-Owned Restaurants
o Characteristics
    o Part of American tradition of family restaurants
    o Publicity is key in gaining attention
    o Chef-owner should get a good backup person

Top Ten American Chef-Owned Restaurants
- o Per Se, New York City, Chef Thomas Keller
- o Daniel, New York City, Chef Daniel Boulud
- o CUT, Palazzo Las Vegas, Las Vegas, Chef Wolfgang Puck
- o Osteria Mozza, Los Angeles, Chefs Mario Batali and Nancy Silverton
- o Morimoto, Philadelphia, Chef Masaharu Morimoto
- o Mesa Grill, Caesars Palace, Las Vegas, Chef Bobby Flay
- o Hamersley's Bistro, Boston Chef Gordon Hamersley
- o NOLA Restaurant, New Orleans, Chef Emeril Lagasse
- o Craftsteak, Las Vegas, Chef Tom Colicchio
- o Olives, Las Vegas, Chef Todd English

Women Chefs as Restaurant Owners
- o Characteristics
  - o Numerous examples
  - o Typical restaurant manager of the future may be a woman
  - o It is agreed that women are more concerned with details, sanitation, and appearance
  - o Women are more likely to be sensitive and empathetic with customers

Celebrity Chefs
- o Bigger today than ever before
  - o Emeril Lagasse
  - o Rachael Ray
  - o Suzanne Goin
  - o Alice Waters
  - o Marc Vetri
  - o Barbara Lynch

Centralized Home Delivery Restaurants
- o Characteristics
  - o Reduces costs of order taking, food preparation, and accounting
  - o Home delivery centers verify and process credit card information
  - o Can be done at any location connected to the Internet, locally or internationally

TRUE OR FALSE QUESTIONS

On the following questions, answer whether the statement provided is true or false.

(T) F 1. Some independent restaurants will grow into small chains, and larger companies will buy out small chains.

(T) F 2. Of the hundreds of types of ethnic restaurants in the United States, Mexican restaurants, boast the largest number.

(T) F 3. Overseas markets constitute a large source of the income of several quick-service chains.

T (F) 4. Centralization increases the costs of order taking, food preparation, and accounting.

(T) F 5. China is divided into culinary districts: Szechuan, Hunan, Cantonese, and northern style.

T (F) 6. Casual dining is less popular than the other types of restaurants because it does not fit the societal trends of a more relaxed lifestyle.

T F 7. Independent restaurants are relatively easy to open; all you need is a few thousand dollars, knowledge of restaurant operations, and a strong desire to succeed.

T F 8. Relations between franchisers and the franchisees are often strained.

T F 9. The first known quick-service restaurant dates back to the 1870s.

T F 10. Family restaurants grew out of the coffee shop-style restaurant.

FILL IN THE BLANKS: KEY TERM REVIEW

On the following questions, fill in the blank with the most appropriate key term.

1. Panera Bread Company and Au Bon Pain are the largest of the chain quick casual . restaurants

2. With_____, an order for pizza could be processed in China and prepared for delivery in New York.

3. One of the main advantages for opening a(n) _____, is that the owner can "do their own thing" in terms of concept development, menus, décor, and so on.

4. The _____ segment includes all restaurants where the food is paid for before service.

5. _____ encompasses a variety of specialized cuisines including Italian, Mexican, and Chinese.

6. Entry into the _____ category of restaurants is appealing to people who may wish to be part of a business that is simplified by a limited menu and that caters to a well-identified market—steak eaters.

7. Defining factors of a(n) _____ include signature food items, creative bar menus or enhanced wine service, and comfortable, homey décor.

8. _____ are built around an idea, usually emphasizing fun and fantasy, glamorizing or romanticizing an activity, such as sports, travel, or an era in time.

9. _____ restaurants defining traits are; the use of high quality ingredients, fresh made to order menu items, healthful options, limited or self-serving formats, upscale décor, and carryout meals.

10. _____ refers to the cuisine and service provided in restaurants where food, drink, and service are expensive, and usually leisurely.

11. _____ restaurants possess the advantage of having an experienced, highly motivated person in charge.

12. _____ are frequently located in or within easy reach of the suburbs and are informal with a simple menu and service designed to appeal to families.

13. _____ have some advantages over independent restaurants, including recognition in the marketplace, greater advertising clout, sophisticated systems development, and discounted purchasing.

MULTIPLE CHOICE QUESTIONS
On the following questions, circle the choice that best answers the question.

1. Franchise restaurants are:
   a. more likely to go "belly up" than independent restaurants
   b. more likely to close down willingly than independent restaurants
   c. less likely to go "belly up" than independent restaurants
   d. more risky than independent restaurants

2. Which of the following concepts has the most sales of all the segment ratings?
   a. Bakery-cafés
   b. Burgers
   c. Mexican
   d. Seafood

3. Meals can be ordered and delivered via the Internet the same way as fresh flowers due to:
   a. centralization
   b. DSL
   c. phone lines
   d. cable

4. If you wish to be part of a business that is simplified by a limited menu and that caters to a well-identified market you may want to open a:
   a. quick service establishment
   b. steakhouse
   c. fine dining establishment
   d. casual dining establishment

5. Which of the following types of restaurants are built around an idea, usually emphasizing fun and fantasy, glamorizing or romanticizing an activity?
   a. Steakhouse
   b. Family
   c. Theme
   d. Seafood

6. Which of the following is a possible option for those who lack extensive restaurant experience and yet want to open up a restaurant with few risks?
   a. Franchise
   b. Manage
   c. Build
   d. Buy

7. Of the hundreds of types of ethnic restaurants in the United States, which type boasts the largest number?
   a. Seafood
   b. Mexican
   c. Chinese
   d. Italian

8. The buy in franchise fee buyers of Jimmy Johns is:
   a. $10,000
   b. $15,000
   c. $25,000
   d. $35,000

9. The average check for fine dining runs _____ or more.
   a. $30
   b. $40
   c. $50
   d. $60

10. Which of the following is the largest seafood chain with $2.7 billion in annual sales, an average sales per restaurant of almost $3.8 million, and 700 restaurants?
    a. The Crab Shack
    b. The Lobster Pot
    c. Red Lobster
    d. Shells

11. Which of the following types of steak is taken from the thick end of the short loin, has a T-bone and a sizable piece of tenderloin?
    a. Porterhouse
    b. Tenderloin
    c. Prime Rib
    d. New York Strip

12. Which of the following is a compact, dense, boneless cut of meat?
    a. T-bone
    b. Porterhouse
    c. Delmonico
    d. New York Strip

13. Which of the following is a small, often boned steak taken from the front section of the short loin?
    a. T-bone
    b. Porterhouse
    c. Delmonico
    d. New York Strip

14. The first known quick-service restaurant dates back to the 1870s, when a New York City foodservice establishment called the:
    a. Plate House
    b. Grand Tavern
    c. Subway.
    d. Delmonico's

15. In the recent past, most food-service millionaires have been:
    a. managers
    b. builders
    c. buyers
    d. franchisers

16. Pizza is native to _____, and it was there that many American soldiers, during World War II, learned to enjoy it.
    a. Rome
    b. Naples
    c. Paris
    d. Lyon

17. Which chef owns the restaurant No. 9 Park, in Boston's Beacon Hill neighborhood?
    a. Suzanne Goin
    b. Alice Waters
    c. Marc Vetri
    d. Barbara Lynch

18. Who might be called a kitchen philosopher whose writing reemphasizes the importance of using only the freshest locally grown organic and seasonal produce and animals that have been raised in a humane, wholesome manner?
    a. Suzanne Goin
    b. Alice Waters
    c. Marc Vetri
    d. Rachel Ray

19. Who is the chef-owner of Spago?
    a. Emeril Lagasse
    b. Wolfgang Puck
    c. Charlie Trotter
    d. Ina Garten

20. Coffeehouses originally were created based on the model of:
    a. French cafés
    b. Irish pubs
    c. Italian bars
    d. French bakeries

21. Luxury hotels can be counted on to have restaurants with well trained and experienced?
    a. bar tenders
    b. porters
    c. dishwashers
    d. chefs

22. This type of restaurant only appears only for a few days, with up front price.
    a. Food truck
    b. Pop ups
    c. Catering service
    d. Fast food

23. Who is the owner of Per Se in New York City?
    a. Wolfgang Puck
    b. Bobby Flay
    c. Thomas Keller
    d. Mario Batali

24. Which of the following has high labor, most profit from wine sales, expensive menu items and costly appointments?
    a. Theme
    b. Food trucks
    c. Family style
    d. Fine Dining

SHORT ANSWER QUESTIONS

1. Name three advantages of opening a chain restaurant.

2. Name three defining traits and give several examples of quick-casual restaurants.

3. Explain the advantages of franchising a restaurant.

4. Describe the advantages and disadvantages of chef-owned restaurants.

5. Describe the advantages for independent restaurateurs.

INTERNET EXERCISE

1. Search the Internet to find the startup costs for two franchises of your choice. List the fees in a table. Do they vary greatly? If so, can you think of reasons why this may be?

ACTIVITY

1. Develop a concept for a regional theme restaurant and answer the following questions:
    o Which type of theme did you choose?
    o Where will the restaurant be located?
    o What types of regional or local items will the menu offer?
    o What type of décor will the restaurant have?
    o Who is your target market?

CHAPTER 3:
CONCEPT, LOCATION, AND DESIGN

INTRODUCTION

The concept should reflect the requirements of the market and location menu; service and decor should complement the concept. Successful concepts exist for both independent and chain restaurants. Some concepts that were successful are now no longer in use. This suggests that fads come and go. Many so-called gimmick restaurants have stood the test of time. The restaurant life cycle varies from a few weeks to several years. The more focused the concept is on a target market, the greater the chance of success. Concepts often must change to keep in step with changing markets and economic conditions. The sequence of restaurant development has many steps between concept and operation. A mission statement will help keep the restaurant operation on a straight course of action toward a common goal.

OBJECTIVES

After reading and studying this chapter, you should be able to:
- o Recognize the benefits of a good restaurant name.
- o Explain the relationship between concept and market.
- o Explain why a restaurant concept might fail.
- o Discuss some qualities of successful restaurant concepts.
- o Identify factors to consider when choosing a restaurant's location.
- o Identify factors to consider when developing a restaurant concept.
- o List restaurant knockout criteria.

CHAPTER OUTLINE

Restaurant Concepts
- o Matrix of ideas
    - o Constitute what will be perceived as the restaurant's image
    - o Should fit a definite target market
    - o Distinguishes the establishment as D&B, different and better, than the competition
    - o May be necessary to modify as competition arises
    - o Best concepts are often the result of learning from mistakes

- o Tips
    - o Make it different enough from the competition
    - o Don't let it be too far ahead of current times
    - o Don't price your menu out of the market
    - o Pay attention to food costs

- o Make your concept profitable
- o Good concepts are on-trend
- o Make your concept easily identifiable
- o Take inspiration from others
- o Make sure the concept and location fit
- o Love your concept

Concepts: Clear Cut or Ambiguous?
- o Many restaurants lack clear cut concepts
  - o No integration of the atmospherics
  - o Everything should fit together:
- o Concept is strengthened if it establishes an identity
- o The name of the restaurant is part of the image.
- o The restaurant name can tell the customer what to anticipate

Protecting a Restaurant's Name
- o Lawsuits over names happen
  - o If another party uses your name you should take action
  - o Loss of the right to a name means changing signs, menus, promotional material, etc.
  - o It can mean court costs and, perhaps, loss of power that has been built into the name by the superior operator

The McDonald's Concept and Image
- o Greatest restaurant success story of all time
  - o Concept: all-American family restaurant
  - o Simple, straightforward menu

Defining the Concept and Market
- o Selecting a concept
  - o Define it precisely in the context of which markets will find it appealing
  - o Market may constitute a small percentage of the total population
- o There must be a market to support the concept
  - o Market gap and need for the concept offered

Successful Restaurant Concepts
- o Stays close to the guest and concentrates on quality and service
- o Examples
  - o TGI Friday's
  - o Spago
  - o Planet Hollywood
  - o Lettuce Entertain You Enterprises
  - o Corner Bakery Café
  - o Union Square Hospitality Group
  - o Parallel 33
- o Hard Rock Café- one of most successful restaurant chains

- o Danny Meyer: A restaurant success story
  - o Union Square Hospitality Group

Restaurant Life Cycles
- o Nearly all restaurants have an almost human life cycle: birth, growth, maturity, senescence, and death.
  - o Familial lack of enthusiasm
  - o Changing demographics
  - o Fashions change

Concept Adaptation
- o Concepts that have not been tested
  - o Most need some adaptation to the particular market
- o Concept development has always been important in the industry
  - o Becoming more so now that dining districts are developing in almost every community
- o Different menus and prices attract different markets

Changing or Modifying a Concept
- o Many highly successful concepts that have worked well for years gradually turn sour
  - o Customer base and demographics change
  - o Morale and personal service may decline

Copy and improve
- o Every concept is built on ideas from other concepts
  - o Modifications and changes, new combinations, and changes in design, layout, menu, and service
  - o Creative copycats may borrow ideas from a number of operations

When a Concept Fails
- o Concept can be changed to fit the market
  - o Conversion can take place while the restaurant is doing business
- o Name, decor, and menu can be changed
  - o Customers who have left may return if the new concept appeals to them
  - o New concept may better appeal to the same market

Restaurant Symbology
- o Includes the logo, line drawings, linen napkins, and service uniforms
  - o All helps to create the atmosphere
  - o Take cues from larger companies to come up with symbols and signs that reflect the restaurant's concept

Multiple-Concept Chains
- o Can have five or more restaurants in the same block
  - o Each competing with the others
  - o Each acquiring a part of the restaurant market
- o Tricon Global Restaurants, Inc.
  - o Largest of all restaurant companies
  - o Three concepts: KFC, Taco Bell, and Pizza Hut

Sequence of Restaurant Development: From concept to opening
- o Sequence of events may include the following 15 steps:
  - o Choosing a location
  - o Business marketing initiated
  - o Layout and equipment planned
  - o Menu determined
  - o First architectural sketches made
  - o Licensing and approvals sought
  - o Financing arranged
  - o Working blueprints developed
  - o Contracts let for bidding
  - o Contractor selected
  - o Construction or remodeling begun
  - o Furnishing and equipment ordered
  - o Key personnel hired
  - o Hourly employees selected and trained
  - o Restaurant opened

Planning Services
- o Many aspects of design are carried out by other parties
  - o Designers perform many services

Common Denominators of Restaurants
- o Some common factors
  - o Human needs met by the restaurant
  - o Menu prices
  - o Degree of service offered
  - o Space provided for each customer
  - o Rate of seat turnover
  - o Advertising and promotions expenditures
  - o Productivity per employee
  - o Labor and food costs

Utility versus pleasure
- o Include
  - o What is the purpose of a particular restaurant
  - o Pleasure dining increases as service, atmosphere, and quality of food increases.
  - o Pleasure increases as menu price increases

Degree of Service Offered

- Restaurant service varies from none at all to a maximum in a high style luxury restaurant.
  - Vending machines impersonal-no service at all.
  - Luxury restaurant, captain and two bus-persons may attend each table
  - Customer pays for food, also the ambience and attention of service personnel.
- Seven categories of service:
  - Vending
  - Quick service
  - Fast casual
  - Casual
  - Family restaurant
  - Dinner house
  - Luxury restaurant

Time of Eating and Seat Turnover

- The seat turnover and speed of eating correlate with the restaurant classification but not perfectly.
- Turnover is also highly correlated with the efficiency of the operation.

Square Food Requirements

- Amount of space per customer needed by each type of restaurant

Menu Price and Cost per Seat

- Menu pricing correlates highly with the degree of service offered, the time of eating, the labor cost the amount of space offered the customer and cost of the restaurant itself.

Correct Number of Seats

- Theoretically a given location will support a given number of seats with a particular concept.
- Surveys show that 40 to 50 percent of all table service customers arrive in pairs;30 percent come alone or in parties of three, and 20 percent in groups of four or more.
- It is better to build too small than too large

Advertising and Promotion Expenditures

- Expenditures may vary according to the type of restaurant

Labor Costs as a Percentage of Sales

- Productivity per employee correlates highly with the various elements, moving from a high point at quick service to a low point in a luxury restaurant.
- Labor costs vary inversely with productivity.

Planning Decisions that Relate to Concept Development

- Who are the target markets, the customers?
- Buy, Build, Lease or Franchise?
- Food preparation from scratch or from convenience Items?
- Limited or extensive menu?

- o How much service, limited or full?
- o Young part-time employees or older career employees?
- o Paid advertising or word-of-mouth advertising?
- o Grand or quiet opening?
- o Electricity or gas?

Profitability
- o Most profitable restaurants are in the quick service category.
- o Oddly enough, few restaurant management students opt for quick-service management, believing it lacks the variety, glamor and opportunity for self-expression.
- o Investor cares most about profitability and maximized profits.

The Mission Statement
- o Encapsulates objectives for the business
    - o Can be brief, encompassing, and/or explicit
- o Elements
    - o Purpose of the business and the nature of what it offers
    - o Business goals, objectives, and strategies
    - o Philosophies and values the business and employees follow

Concept and Location
- o Good location depends on the
    - o Kind of restaurant
    - o Clientele
    - o Size of potential market
    - o Price structure

Criteria for Locating a Restaurant
- o Criteria for locating a restaurant
    - o *Restaurant Business* Magazine
- o Selecting a restaurant sit or a restaurant city is both a science and an art.
    - o More important is the amount and intensity of competition already existing.

Location Criteria
- o Includes
    - o Demographics of the area
    - o Visibility from a major highway
    - o Accessibility from a major highway
    - o Number of potential customers passing by the restaurant
    - o Distance from the potential market
    - o Desirability of surroundings

Some Restaurants Create Their Own Location
o Dinner or family-style restaurants
    o Need not place the same high priority on convenience of location

Sources of location information
o Location decisions
o Real estate agents are prime sources

Traffic Generators
o Look for built-in traffic generators, such as hotels, business parks, in-door arenas, theaters, retail centers, and residential neighborhoods.

Knockout Criteria
o Includes
    o Proper zoning
    o Drainage, sewage, utilities
    o Minimal size
    o Short lease
    o Excessive traffic speed
    o Access from a highway or street
    o Visibility from both sides of the street

Other Location Criteria
o Includes
    o Market population
    o Family income
    o Growth or decline of the area
    o Competition from comparable restaurants
    o Restaurant row or cluster concept

Suburban, Nook-and-Cranny, and Shopping Mall Locations
o Restaurants do well in a variety of locations
    o Depends on menu and style of operation

Minimum population needed
o New, fairly inexpensive, food is in the American menu stream and is where the people assemble.

Downtown versus suburban
o New restaurants continually displace old ones.

Average travel time to reach restaurants
o Most diners-out select restaurants that are close by

Matching location with concept
o Size of the lot, visibility, availability of parking, access from roads, etc. all have an impact on style of restaurant that will fit a location.

Restaurant Chain Location Specifications
- o Critical criteria
  - o Metropolitan area with 50,000 population
  - o 20,000 cars per 24 hour period
  - o Residential backup, plus motels, shopping centers or office parks.
  - o Minimum 200 foot frontage
  - o Area demonstrating growth and stability
  - o Easy access and visibility
  - o Availability of all utilities to the property, including sewer

Takeover locations
- o Beginning restaurateur often starts by leasing or buying out an existing restaurant.

Restaurant topographical surveys
- o Using town or city map and plotting the location of existing restaurants on the map.

Cost of the location
- o Can the concept and the potential market support the location selected?

Visibility, Accessibility, and Design Criteria
- o Visibility and accessibility
  - o Important criteria for any restaurant
- o Design
  - o Needs to correlate with the theme

Location Information Checklist
- o Dimensions and total square footage
- o Linear footage
- o Distance and direction
- o Average 24 hour traffic
- o Number of moving traffic lanes
- o Traffic controls
- o Posted speed limits
- o On-street parking
- o Parking requirements
- o Landscaping and setback
- o Topography
- o Type of soil
- o Drainage
- o Existing structures
- o Type of energy available
- o Sewers
- o Underground utilities
- o Present zoning classifications
- o Use and zoning of adjacent property
- o Building limitations

- o Character of surrounding area
- o Population and Income characteristics
- o Agencies requiring plan approval
- o Status of annexation
- o Signage
- o Construction codes
- o Restaurant competition
- o Offering price of property

TRUE OR FALSE QUESTIONS

On the following questions, answer whether the statement provided is true or false.

T   F   1. Most restaurant concepts that have not been tested need some adaptation to the particular market.

T   F   2. Concept development has always been important in the restaurant industry, but it is becoming more so now that dining districts are developing in almost every community.

T   F   3. Loss of the right to use a name means changing signs, menus, and promotional material.

T   F   4. If the operator is competent, they should sell their restaurant if it is failing.

T   F   5. Turnover is slightly correlated with the efficiency of the operation.

T   F   6. There is no such thing as a completely new restaurant concept.

T   F   7. Up to 50 percent of the meals eaten away from home are for utilitarian purposes, while the other 90 percent are for pleasure.

T   F   8. McDonald's is a multiple concept chain.

T   F   9. You should never name a restaurant after its owner.

T   F   10. The best guide in selecting a planner/consultant is that person's experience and reputation.

KEY TERM FILL IN THE BLANKS: KEY TERM REVIEW

For the following questions, fill in the blank with the most appropriate key term.

1.   Using a town or city map and plotting the location of existing restaurants on the map, is an example of a(n) _____.

2. The matrix of ideas that constitutes what will be perceived as the restaurant's image is the _____.

3. A(n) _____ should include a vision of what the restaurant owner would like for the restaurant in the future.

4. If another party uses your restaurant name, you should _____, take action against that person by proving that you, the challenging party, used the name first.

5. When opening a new restaurant you should try to develop a concept better suited to its market than that presented by competing restaurants. This is known as being _____.

6. From the time a concept is put together, until a location is obtained, there is a(n) _____ of restaurant development.

7. Without a doubt, the most _____ restaurants are in quick-service category.

8. The _____ offered probably correlates with menu price and pleasure—at least, that is the expectation of the diner.

9. Up to 75 percent of the meals eaten away from home are for_____ purposes, while the other 25 percent are for_____.

MULTIPLE CHOICE QUESTIONS: CONCEPT REVIEW
On the following questions, circle the choice that best answers the question.

1. The best concepts are often the result of:
   a. learning from mistakes
   b. franchising
   c. building new
   d. managing

2. People often spend about ____ minutes travel time when going to a cafeteria or department store restaurant.
   a. 5
   b. 10
   c. 15
   d. 20

3. A concept created by Lettuce Entertain You Enterprises is:
   a. Papagus
   b. Corner Bakery Café
   c. Hard Rock Café
   d. Automat

4. Concepts comprise:
   a. advertising only
   b. everything that affects how the patron views the restaurant
   c. promotion only
   d. everything that affects how the worker views the restaurant

5. The best guide in selecting a planner/consultant is that persons:
   a. demeanor
   b. way of dressing
   c. experience and reputation
   d. overall appearance

6. The space allocation for backstage is usually _____ of the total square footage, depending on the type of restaurant.
   a. 10%
   b. 20%
   c. 30%
   d. 40%

7. Surveys show that 40 to 50 percent of all table-service restaurant customers arrive in:
   a. groups of 4
   b. groups of 3 or more
   c. pairs
   d. singles

8. Symbols are:
   a. seen in the sign, logo, colors, upholstery, and lighting of the restaurant
   b. not seen in the sign, logo, colors, upholstery, and lighting of the restaurant
   c. are not part of the concept
   d. are not used in developing a restaurant

9. Without a doubt, the most profitable restaurants are in the:
   a. steakhouse category
   b. fast food category
   c. fine dining category
   d. quick-service category

10. The magazine *Restaurant Business* publishes an annual *Restaurant Growth Index*, the purpose of which is to list:
    a. all the new restaurants that opened in the United States
    b. the best and worst places to open a restaurant in the United States
    c. new restaurant job openings
    d. all the new restaurants that opened in the major cities of the United States

11. Which of the following is the prime source of information for restaurant location decisions?
a. potential customers
b. the IRS
c. real estate agents
d. newspapers

12. Generally, restaurant patrons will travel an average of _____ minutes to reach a hotel, steak, full-menu, or fish restaurant.
a. 5 to 10
b. 11 to 15
c. 15 to 18
d. 18 to 25

13. The logo, line drawings, linen napkins, and the service uniforms are all part of:
a. restaurant symbology
b. the market
c. accessibility
d. visibility

14. Concept development has always been important in the restaurant industry, it is now becoming:
a. less so in todays market due to the declining economy
b. more so now that dining districts are developing in almost every community
c. nearly impossible due to the population explosion
d. impossible to do, since the market is always changing

15. The concept is devised to interest a certain group of people, called a:
a. market matrix
b. diverse population
c. operational market mix
d. target market

16. When locating a chain restaurant, how many cars per 24 hour period should pass by the business?
a. 5,000
b. 10,000
c. 20,000
d. 40,000

17. The greatest restaurant success story of all time is that of:
a. Wendy's
b. McDonalds
c. KFC
d. Pizza Hut

18. Who is the president of Union Square Hospitality Group?
    a. Danny Meyer
    b. Peter Morton
    c. Ray Kroc
    d. Robert Butterfield

19. Restaurant chains with preplanned restaurant concepts generally reduce the opening timeline by _____ months.
    a. 1 to 3
    b. 3 to 6
    c. 4 to 7
    d. 6 to 12

20. The extent to which the restaurant can be seen for a reasonable amount of time, whether the potential guest is walking or driving is the concept of:
    a. accessibility
    b. visibility
    c. topography
    d. zoning

21. All restaurants go through periods of staff or familial lack of enthusiasm, changing demographics and changes in fashion. This is called?
    a. Trending
    b. Life cycle
    c. Business model
    d. Shake out period

22. When developing a restaurant from conception to completion, what is the first step?
    a. Menu determined
    b. Key personnel hired
    c. Contracts let for bidding
    d. Choosing a location

23. Built-in traffic generators for enhanced business would be?
    a. Large open fields
    b. A prison located close to the restaurant
    c. Retail centers and shopping mall
    d. Large farming operation

SHORT ANSWER QUESTIONS

1. What is the 15-step sequence of restaurant development?

2. Name five services a designer performs.

3. Describe three reasons the most profitable restaurants are in the quick-service category?

4. List the "knockout criteria" for selecting a location.

INTERNET EXERCISE

1. Go to the Nation's Restaurant News Web site. Provide a summary for three of the latest headlines.

ACTIVITY

1. Create a flow chart containing the sequence of restaurant development provided in the chapter and provide two examples of actions that must be taken during each of the steps.

CHAPTER 4:
THE MENU

INTRODUCTION

Menus and menu planning are the most crucial elements of the restaurant. The many considerations in menu planning help us realize the scope and depth of general planning necessary for successful operation. The two main approaches to menu pricing strategies are comparative and individual dish costing. Contribution margins vary from item to item, with the higher food-cost percentage items yielding the greater contribution margin. The various types of menus and menu items are discussed, together with menu design and layout.

OBJECTIVES

After reading and studying this chapter, you should be able to:
- o   Identify factors to consider when planning a menu.
- o   List and describe some common menu types.
- o   Discuss methods for determining menu item pricing.
- o   Identify factors to consider when determining a menu's design and layout.

CHAPTER OUTLINE

The Menu
- o   Heart of any restaurant
    - o   Showcases everything you have to offer for food and beverage
- o   Dos and Don'ts of menu planning:
    - o   Check out the competitions' menus and websites.
    - o   Ask yourself, how will my restaurant and menu be different from and better than the others?
    - o   The theme of the menu, its design and colors, should reflect the theme and Décor of the restaurant.
    - o   Use a clear, easy-to-read font like Times New Roman 14 point so guests can read the menu.
    - o   Have a couple of focus groups read your menu and give you feedback.
    - o   Incorporate local names into the descriptions of dishes.
    - o   Specialty menu items can have a star or other insignia to draw attention to Them.
    - o   Use a symbol for potential ingredients that may trigger allergies in guests, such as peanuts or eggs.
    - o   For the layout, use one or two columns, not more, as the menu will look too crowded.

- o Don't use the clipart that comes as part of your computer software; your menu will look as if it was done at home. Pay for the rights to use the art
- o Don't use too much technical jargon. Keep it simple
- o Avoid saying exactly how many pieces of food come in a dish.
- o Don't laminate your menu. Instead invest in menu jackets.

Consideration in Planning a Menu
- o One of the most important factors for patrons is the quality of food.
- o Considerations in menu planning include
    - o Capability of cooks and consistency of preparation
    - o Equipment capacity and layout
    - o Seasonal availability of menu ingredients
    - o Price and pricing strategy
    - o Nutritional value
    - o Accuracy in menu
    - o Menu items
    - o Menu types
    - o Menu engineering
    - o Menu design and layout
    - o Standardized recipes
    - o Menu trends
- o Menu is the most important part of the restaurant concept.

Capability/Consistency
- o Capability to produce the quality and quantity of food necessary
    - o Basic consideration
- o Standardized recipes
    - o Ensures consistency
- o Elements that have an effect on capability and consistency
    - o Menu complexity
    - o Number of meals served
    - o Number of people to supervise

Equipment Capacity and Layout
- o Equipment must be installed in an efficient layout
    - o Systematic flow of items from receiving clerk to guests
- o Avoid overuse
    - o Too many items requiring one piece of equipment

Availability of Ingredients
- o Constant, reliable source of supply at a reasonable price must be established
    - o Take advantage of seasonal items when they are at their lowest price and best quality
    - o High-quality ingredients make a high quality product

Price and Pricing Strategy
Price is a major factor in men selection.
- o   Factors in building price-value
  - o   Amount of product
  - o   Quality of product
  - o   Reliability or consistency of product
  - o   Uniqueness of product
  - o   Product options or choices
  - o   Service convenience
  - o   Comfort level
  - o   Reliability or consistency of service
  - o   Tie-in offers or freebies

Factors in Pricing
- o   Menu items
  - o   Selected to complement the restaurant image
  - o   Appeal to its target market

Menu Pricing Strategies
- o   Comparative approach
  - o   Analyze competitions' prices and determine menu
- o   Ratio method
  - o   Price individual item and multiply by ratio amount necessary to achieve desired food-cost percentage
  - o   May lead to weighted average approach

Calculating Food-Cost Percentage
- o   Food cost
  - o   Reflected in pricing
  - o   Varies with sales
  - o   Provides a simple target to aim for
  - o   Barometer of the profitability of the restaurant
- o   Opening Inventory + purchases - closing inventory = cost of goods sold
- o   Taking a food inventory is time-consuming and complicated

Contribution Margin
- o   Difference between sales price and cost of item
  - o   Amount left over goes towards covering fixed and variable costs
- o   Example
  - o   Steak selling price: $14.95
  - o   Steak cost: $ 5.00
  - o   Contribution margin: $9.95

Nutritional Value
- o   Guests are becoming increasingly concerned about the nutritional value of food.
  - o   Demand for healthier items like chicken and fish is increasing

- o Prompted a change in cooking methods
- o Boiling, poaching, steaming, roasting, etc. as opposed to frying
- o Changes in type of cooking oil
- o Lower-fat menu items
- o Increased numbers serving vegetarian, vegan and raw fare

Gluten-Free Cooking and Menu Items
- o It is important for restaurants to stay current with food allergies and intolerances.
- o The gluten-free diet stems from a certain percentage of the population that is unable to process a particular protein.

Food Allergy Safety Precautions and Staff Properly Trained to Handle Attacks.
- o Up to 50 million Americans *an allergy* which causes various reactions, *affecting* a *person's* eyes, nose, throat, lungs, skin, or *gastrointestinal tract.*
  - o The staff should be tested on all ingredients
  - o Most important, communication between the guest, server, and chef must be present.

Veganism and Vegetarianism and Raw Foods Diet
- o Many people and cultures in the world practice veganism and vegetarianism
  - o Vegan-only plants and vegetables
  - o Vegetarian-plants, vegetables butter, milk, eggs and cheese
- o Challenges faced by vegetarian diet
  - o Heart health challenges
  - o Vitamin B_{12} deficiencies
  - o Iron and calcium deficiencies

Diversity in Diet Plans and Cross-Cultural Preferences
- o Diet plans have been around for thousands of years.
  - o Fad diets
  - o Today's nutritional experts use the term pyramid

Flavor
- o Sensory impression of a food or other substance determined by chemical senses
- o Other factors
  - o Aroma
  - o Texture
  - o Sight
  - o Sound

Accuracy in Menu
- o Restaurants must be accurate and truthful when describing dishes on the menu
  - o Beef described as prime must be prime
- o Some restaurants have been heavily fined for violations of accuracy in menu
- o Menu-labeling calorie count requirement
  - o New York became the first municipality to enact

Menu Items
- o In the interests of sustainability, restaurateurs use local ingredients
  - o Drive the menu at many contemporary restaurants

Menu Items
- o Depend on type of restaurant
- o Steps useful in determining whether to add and item to the menu
  - o Create an objective and a timetable.
  - o Develop a list of possible menu ideas.
  - o Narrow that list down.
  - o Test those ideas with consumers.
  - o Build prototypes.
  - o Internally narrow the prototypes down.
  - o Test and renew the prototypes in selected restaurants.
  - o Put the prototypes on the menu.

Appetizers and soups
- o Six to eight appetizers are adequate for the majority of restaurants

Salads
- o Salads have become the preferred start in a growing number of restaurants

Entrees
- o There should be at least eight entrees.
  - o Item from each of the major meat, pasta, poultry, seafood and fish categories.
  - o Different cooking methods

Desserts
- o May include a selection of fruits, pies, cakes, ices and pastries.

Matching/Pairing with Wine
- o New classics couple a type of wine with a general class of food.
  - o Example: Goat cheese with a Sauvignon Blanc

Menu Types
- o Include
  - o Dinner-house: separate similar entrees
  - o À la carte: individually priced items
  - o Table d'hôte: selection of several dishes from which patrons make a complete meal at a fixed price
  - o Du jour menu: lists items served only on a particular day
  - o Cyclical: generally used in institutions
  - o California: order any menu item at any time of day
  - o Tourist: used to attract tourists
  - o Degustation: sample of the chef's best dishes

Lunch and dinner menus
- o Lunch menus need to be easy to read and food must be produced quickly
- o Dinner menu portions and prices tend to be larger

Degustation (chef's tasting) menus
- o Sample of the chef's best dishes
- o Served in several courses
- o Takes longer to serve

Sustainable Menus
- o Example: Founding Farmers restaurant

Kids' Menu
- o Restaurants that cater to families usually have a separate kids' menu
  - o Bold colors and catchy make-believe characters
- o Other amenities
  - o Play areas
  - o Fun placemats
  - o Crayons
  - o Small take-home prizes

Menu Engineering
- o Several approaches
  - o Must be a balance
  - o Bayou and Bennett recommend analysis
  - o Menu management software applications

Menu Design and Layout
- o Silent salesperson of the restaurant: Should reflect the ambience of the restaurant
  - o Menu size may range from one to several pages
  - o Come in a variety of shapes
  - o Printing and artwork should harmonize with theme of the restaurant
  - o Names of dishes should be easy to read and understand
  - o Should include a strong focal point

Standardized Recipes
- o Used to maintain consistent food quality
  - o Indicates a variety of standards
  - o Acts as a control device

Menu Trends
- o Always linked to the behavior of an entire population
  - o Locally grown and sourced ingredients
  - o Healthy menu items for children
  - o Sustainable food practices
  - o Mobile food business(food trucks)
  - o Culinary cocktails
  - o Smartphone apps

TRUE OR FALSE QUESTIONS

On the following questions, answer whether the statement provided is true or false.

(T) F   1. Professor Jack Miller developed one of the earlier approaches to menu engineering.

T (F) 2. Menus should have no more than two panels.   *Typically 9x12" or 11 by 17"*

T (F) 3. Federal law stipulates that businesses (including restaurants) may not misrepresent what they are selling.

T (F) 4. Vegan restaurants do not serve food heated above 116°F (46.7°C).

(T) F   5. Dinner-house menus separate similar entrées: beef in one section, seafood in another.

(T) F   6. The menu is the most important part of the restaurant concept.

(T) F   7. A table d'hôte menu offers a selection of several dishes from which patrons choose to make a complete meal at a fixed price.

T (F) 8. Four to five appetizers are adequate for the majority of restaurants.   *6 – 7*

T F   9. Operators use food and labor costs as a combination known as prime cost, which should be close to 55% to 60% of sales.

(T) F 10. The standardized recipe lists the quantities of ingredients and features a simple step-by-step method to produce a quality product.

FILL IN THE BLANKS: KEY TERM REVIEW

On the following questions, fill in the blank with the most appropriate key term.

1. The use of standardized recipes and cooking procedures will help ensure the _____Consistency_____ of menu items.

2. There are two basic components of _____ value creation: what you provide and what you charge for it.

3. Restaurant guests, some more than others, are becoming increasingly concerned about the _____nutrition_____ of food, creating a higher demand for healthier items, such as chicken and fish.

4. _____Vegetarian_____ restaurants, such as Radha located in Manhattan, do not serve meat.

5. A constant, reliable source of supply at a reasonable price must be established and maintained, known as _____Availability_____.

6. ___Raw Food___ is not heated above 116°F (46.7°C).

7. ___Accuracy___ in menu means that if the trout on the menu comes from an Idaho trout farm, it cannot be described as coming from a more exotic-sounding location.

8. The ___contribution margin___ is the difference between the sales price and the cost of the item.

9. The ___Capability___ of the chefs or cooks to produce the quality and quantity of food necessary is a basic consideration.

10. Menu ___design___ and ___layout___ have been called the silent salespersons of the restaurant, and overall should reflect the ambiance of the restaurant.

11. ___Vegan___ restaurants exclude everything a vegetarian restaurant excludes, in addition to all dairy products.

12. The cost of ingredients must equal the predetermined ___food-cost___ percentage.

13. In order to produce the desired menu items, the proper ___equipment___ must be installed in an efficient layout.

14. _____ is a management application that takes a deterministic approach in evaluating decisions regarding current and future menu pricing, design, and contents.

15. _____ are selected to avoid overuse of one piece of equipment.

16. The two main types of _____ are the food-cost percentage method and the ratio method.

17. À la carte, table d'hôte, and du jour are examples of ___menus___.

MULTIPLE CHOICE QUESTIONS: CONCEPT REVIEW
On the following questions, circle the choice that best answers the question.

1. Which of the following is the most important ingredient in providing guests with a pleasurable dining experience?
   a. Management
   b. Service
   c. Concept
   d. Menu

2. Which of the following helps ensure *consistency* for the restaurant?
   a. Seasonal ingredients
   b. Concept
   c. Location
   d. Standardized recipes and cooking procedures

3. There are two basic components of value creation:
   a. what you provide and what you charge for it
   b. what you make for profits and what you charge for a product
   c. what you guests want to pay for an item and what you charge for it
   d. none of the above

4. There are two main menu pricing strategies a(n):
   a. relative approach and a comparative approach
   b. individual menu item approach and value perception approach
   c. comparative approach and value perception approach
   d. comparative approach and the individual menu item approach

5. The comparative approach analyzes the:
   a. competition's prices to determine specials
   b. individual menu items and multiplies them by the ratio amount necessary to achieve the required food-cost percentage
   c. competition's prices and determines the menu
   d. seasonal availability of menu items

6. Prime costs of a restaurant should be close to:
   a. 30% to 35% of sales
   b. 40% to 45% of sales
   c. 55% to 60% of sales
   d. 65% to 70% of sales

7. Raw bars or restaurants do not serve food:
   a. above 75°F
   b. below 75°F
   c. above 116°F
   d. below 116°F

8. The difference between the sales price and the cost of the item is called the:
   a. ratio of expenditure
   b. contribution margin
   c. overhead expenses
   d. disbursement margin

9. If total sales were $200,000 for the month, the food cost of $66,666 divided into the $200,000 would produce a food cost of _____.
   a. 15%
   b. 25%
   c. 33%
   d. 47%

10. With grilled salmon, nowadays, the wine of choice seems to be a _____.
   a. Pinot noir
   b. Merlot
   c. Chardonnay
   d. Riesling

11. Vegetarian restaurants:
   a. do not serve dairy
   b. do not serve meat
   c. serve only chicken
   d. do not serve dairy or meat

12. Operators use food and labor costs as a combination known as:
   a. negligible costs
   b. gross costs
   c. real costs
   d. prime costs

13. The cost of ingredients must equal the:
   a. perception of value
   b. predetermined food-cost percentage
   c. most profits
   d. price-value ratio

14. According to the text, the pricing strategy that results in less potential problems is the:
   a. relative approach
   b. the individual menu item approach
   c. comparative approach
   d. value approach

15. Several cities have now banned _____, which are a type of fat.
   a. trans fatty acids
   b. non-hydrogenated fats
   c. glutens
   d. saturated fats

16. If a restaurant offers a steak on the menu that costs $5 and sells for $14.95, the contribution margin is _____ for every steak sold.
   a. $4.95
   b. $5.00
   c. $9.95
   d. $14.95

17. How many appetizers are adequate for the majority of restaurant menus?
    a. 2 to 4
    b. 3 to 5
    c. 6 to 8
    d. 8 to 10

18. Generally, in a table-service restaurant, there should be at least _____ entrées.
    a. 6
    b. 8
    c. 10
    d. 12

19. Baked goat cheese frequently shows up on menus in salads, on a designer pizza, or incorporated into a baked mélange, and the accompanying wine served is a _____.
    a. Sauvignon blanc
    b. Pinot noir
    c. Chardonnay
    d. Chianti

20. Which menu type is a list of food items served only on a particular day?
    a. À la carte
    b. Du jour
    c. Table d'hôte
    d. California

21. No animal or dairy product of any kind is served at this type of restaurant
    a. Raw food
    b. Pescatarian
    c. Vegan
    d. Fructatarian

22. Nutritionists frequently mention "Food Pyramids". Tomatoes, chilies, cumin, garlic and cilantro and would be found in which of the following Pyramid ?
    a. Latino
    b. Asian
    c. Mediterranean
    d. African

SHORT ANSWER QUESTIONS

1. What is a standardized recipe?

2. Name five factors in building price-value?

3. What is the contribution margin?

4. Name four types of menus.

INTERNET EXERCISE

1. Search the Internet for various vegan, vegetarian, and raw fare recipes. Choose one of each recipe type to share with the class. Be sure to consider the availability of ingredients, seasonality, and appeal.

ACTIVITY

1. Choosing from the main menu types discussed in the chapter, create a list of items for sample menu. Be sure to include appetizers, entrées, and desserts using the guidelines discussed. Next, add wines that would be appropriately paired with your menu items.

CHAPTER 5:

PLANNING AND EQUIPPING THE KITCHEN

INTRODUCTION

Kitchen planning precedes equipment purchasing. The kitchen plan helps ensure an easy flow of food in and out of the kitchen. The idea is to place the equipment in such a way that the distance between it and the staff members who use it is minimized. Planners may also recommend equipment that fits the menu and the restaurants' clientele and make sure that the chef and kitchen crew have the knowledge and skills to operate the kitchen. The purposes, uses, limitations, and prices of restaurant equipment are discussed. Decreasing energy use is another result of good kitchen planning and equipment selection.

OBJECTIVES

After reading and studying this chapter, you should be able to:
- o Identify factors to consider when planning a kitchen's layout.
- o Discuss the benefits and drawbacks of an open kitchen.
- o Explain selection factors for purchasing kitchen equipment.
- o Identify various cooking techniques.

CHAPTER OUTLINE

Kitchen Planning
- o Involves the allocation of space within the kitchen based on
    - o Equipment needs
    - o Spatial relationships within the kitchen
    - o Need to keep traffic flow to a minimum
- o Overall objective
    - o Minimize number of steps taken by wait staff and kitchen personnel
- o Efficiency and comfort of the staff is important to operation
    - o Servers will take the shortest and most convenient route
    - o Chefs want their work organized to minimize excess activity and unnecessary steps
- o Ergonomics
    - o Applied science of equipment design intended to reduce staff fatigue and discomfort
- o Legislation and public policy also affect foodservice design
    - o Standards to accommodate workers and customers who are disabled
- o Designers must understand the National Sanitation Foundation standards
    - o Apply them to actions of workers
- o Avery suggests these methods of increasing kitchen efficiency

- o Use purveyors that have a wide base of supply
- o Use conveyors to take food to service areas
- o Place service stations in dining rooms with items to reduce back-and-forth traffic
- o Use automatic conveyors to take racks from dining room, through the dishwasher, and back to dining room

Back of the House Green
- o Ways to cut utility costs
  - o Induction ovens
  - o High-speed ovens
- o Purchasing equipment wisely
  - o Can cut energy costs 10 to 30%
- o Exhaust hoods
  - o High-energy user

Open Kitchen
- o Highlights the kitchen or equipment
  - o Standard food preparation: not usually featured
  - o Some use under the counter refrigerator units to conserve space
  - o Area set aside for open kitchens costs about 25% more
- o Drawbacks
  - o Noise level
  - o Dining and banquet rooms
  - o Chefs and cooks are completely exposed to customers

Kitchen Floor Coverings
- o Usually covered with quarry tile, marble, terrazzo, asphalt tile, or sealed concrete
  - o Nonabsorbent, easy to clean, and resistant to abrasive cleaners
- o Neoprene matting
  - o Provides traction in water accumulation areas
- o Should be covered with nonskid materials
  - o Number-one cause of restaurant accidents is slipping and falling

Kitchen Equipment
- o Today, there are advancing trends in sustainable kitchen equipment
  - o Energy Star program
- o National Restaurant Association
  - o Recommendations for reducing water and electricity waste

Categories of Kitchen Equipment
- o Divided according to purpose:
  - o Receiving and storing food
  - o Fabricating and preparing food
  - o Preparing and processing food
  - o Assembling, holding, and serving food
  - o Cleaning up and sanitizing the kitchen and kitchenware

Select the Right Equipment
- o Common questions
    - o Which will be the most efficient for the menu, item by item, and for future items?
    - o What is the equipment's purchase cost and operating cost?
    - o Should the equipment be gas or electric?
    - o Will it produce the food fast enough?
    - o Is it better to buy a large unit or two or more smaller units?
    - o Are replacement parts and service readily available?
    - o Is reliable, used equipment available?
    - o Is more energy-efficient equipment available?

Match Equipment with Menu and Production Schedule
- o Variables
    - o Projected volume of sales for each menu item
    - o Fixed or changing menu
    - o Menu size
    - o Speed of service desired
    - o Nutritional awareness
    - o Equipment selected

Total Cost Versus Original Cost
- o Include
    - o Initial cost
    - o Life expectancy and parts replacement
    - o Cost of energy of each piece of equipment
    - o Cost of warm-up time

Selecting the most efficient equipment for the people and skills available
- o Select only pieces of equipment that are most efficient and necessary.

Deskilling the job with equipment
- o New equipment is designed to reduce or eliminate cooking skills.
    - o Conveyor broiler
    - o Conveyor pizza oven
    - o Automatic crepe machine
    - o Grooved griddle
    - o Cook chill
    - o Sous vide

Equipment Stars
- o Are selected to best prepare the principle menu item

Stove/oven
- o **Most prominent piece of equipment is traditional range.**
    - o Biggest energy user
    - o Kitchen often planned around the stove/oven

Deep-frying equipment
- o Fryers designed for water boiling as well as deep fat frying
- o Pressure fryers

Low temperature ovens
- o Alto Sham

Forced-air convection ovens
- o Fan or rotor makes for rapid circulation and quicker heating of the food.

Microwave ovens
- o Cooks by radiated energy to penetrate the food.
- o Cooking is not uniform
- o Excellent for reheating food

Advantages and disadvantages of microwave cooking
- o Reheat
- o Defrost
- o Precooking
- o Too fast/food under or over cooked
- o Low capacity

Infrared cooking equipment
- o Infrared waves use to reduce cooking time
- o Food can be cooked on both sides at the same time

Hot-food holding tables
- o Heated by gas, electric or steam elements controlled by a thermostat

Refrigerators
- o Reach-ins
- o Walk-ins

Freezers
- o Reach-ins
- o Walk-ins
- o Blast chillers

Ice machines
- o Used to produce ice for ice water and beverages

Pasta-making machines
- o For restaurants that make their own pasta

Specialty cooking equipment
- o Cheese melter

- o Spin dryer
- o Quartz fired oven
- o Induction stove
- o Crepe-making machine

Evaporative coolers
- o Evaporative coolers installed in kitchens reduce the cost of cooling considerably.

Other Cooking Equipment
- o Numerous other kitchen items are available that may be useful for a particular menu
  - o Ice cream holding units, display cases, cream dispensers, meat patty–making machines, garbage disposals, infrared heating lamps, drink dispensers, dough dividers, bakers' stoves, etc.

Maintaining Kitchen Equipment
- o A little like preventive medicine
  - o By following certain practices, major problems can be avoided
- o Restaurant equipment
  - o Generally thought to have a life expectancy of about ten years

Meeting with the Health Inspector
- o Public health officials and planning boards
  - o Want to assure the public that eating in restaurants under their jurisdiction is safe
- o Requirements vary from place to place
  - o Floor drainage systems, exhaust ductwork, distances between dining room tables, seats permitted, parking spaces required, entrances and exits to the parking area and restaurant

TRUE OR FALSE QUESTIONS
On the following questions, answer whether the statement provided is true or false.

T   F   1. The microwave oven has high value for producing baked-dough items and any type of food that involves a leavening action.

T   F   2. Kitchen floors are usually covered with quarry tile, marble, terrazzo, asphalt tile, or sealed concrete.

T   F   3. Ergonomics is the applied science of equipment design intended to reduce staff fatigue and discomfort.

T   F   4. In a full-service restaurant, stovetops, ovens, and broilers are the dominate pieces of kitchen equipment.

T   F   5. Open kitchens are decreasing in popularity due to various disadvantages.

T   F   6. The microwave oven should never be used in a restaurant kitchen.

T   F   7. Carpeting in kitchens is permitted by building codes, but not advisable.

T   F   8. The number-one cause of restaurant accidents is slipping and falling.

T   F   9. The area set aside for open kitchens costs about 10% more than a standard kitchen.

T   F   10. An overall objective of layout planning is to minimize the number of steps taken by wait staff and kitchen personnel.

FILL IN THE BLANKS: KEY TERM REVIEW

On the following questions, fill in the blank with the most appropriate key term.

1. A(n) _____ or _____ can be thought of as two boxes, one inside the other, separated by insulation.

2. Food is prepared and rapidly chilled to prevent bacterial growth and is available in portions of various sizes. This is called the _____ method.

3. Cutting out only one hour each day of _____ "on" time can translate to a savings of around $450 annually.

4. _____ with ovens is often done during the night, which frees up oven space for daytime use.

5. _____, which permit low-temperature roasting and baking, are widely used in the restaurant business to reduce shrinkage of meat and to hold meat so that it can be served to order from the oven.

6. Important pieces of cooking equipment are the oven, tilting skillet, combination convection and _____, convection steam cooker, the microwave oven, and the deep fryer.

7. Directions for baking with a(n) _____ oven must be followed exactly; otherwise some foods, such as sheet cakes, will dry out excessively on top.

8. The _____ technique is when food is prepared, individually vacuum packed, and refrigerated for future use.

9. Operators use _____ to boil seafood, vegetables, and pasta products.

10. A(n) _____ is similar to a conventional oven except that a fan or rotor, usually located in the back, makes for rapid circulation of the air, which results in quicker heating of the food.

11. Combination _____ allow cooks to use either moist or dry heat, or a combination of both.

12. Dr. Arthur C. Avery studied kitchen efficiency and created arrangements of _____ in a typical service restaurant that has a fairly limited menu.

13. The _____ machines operate with water temperatures as low as 100°F.

14. With the availability of convection ovens, steam-jacketed kettles, and _____, some kitchen planners deliberately eliminate the range, regarding it as cumbersome and inefficient.

15. Today, there are advancing trends in sustainable _____.

MULTIPLE CHOICE QUESTIONS: CONCEPT REVIEW
On the following questions, circle the choice that best answers the question.

1. The area set aside for open kitchens costs about _____ more than in a standard kitchen.
   a. 10%
   b. 15%
   c. 20%
   d. 25%

2. Which of the following pieces of kitchen equipment permits low-temperature roasting and baking?
   a. Hot food holding tables
   b. Microwaves
   c. Low-temperature ovens
   d. Forced-air convection oven

3. Because microwaves are absorbed preferentially by water:
   a. they should not be used in restaurants
   b. cooking is not uniform
   c. heat is slowly conducted into the interior
   d. always cover food with plastic wrap

4. The _____ program is a joint program of the U.S. Environmental Protection Agency and the U.S. Department of Energy.
   a. LEED
   b. Energy Star
   c. LIHEAP
   d. U.S. DOE Energy Efficiency

5. Evaporative coolers installed in kitchens:
   a. reduce the cost of cooling considerably where humidity in the outside air is low
   b. reduce the cost of cooling considerably where humidity in the outside air is high
   c. overall increase the cost of cooling
   d. are not recommended

6. Restaurant equipment is generally thought to have a life expectancy of about:
   a. one year
   b. three years
   c. seven years
   d. ten years

7. Infrared wavelengths used for cooking are only microns in length. Wavelengths of about _____ microns are said to be the most effective for cooking foods.
   a. 0 to 1
   b. 1.4 to 5
   c. 5 to 6.14
   d. 7 to 10.14

8. According to the text, after being purchased restaurant equipment may drop as much as _____ in value.
   a. 80%
   b. 85%
   c. 90%
   d. 95%

9. The menu determines the:
   a. staff
   b. equipment
   c. location
   d. concept

10. McDonald's restaurants are built around the:
    a. griddle
    b. convection oven
    c. deep fryer
    d. a and c

11. Food is individually vacuum-packed and refrigerated for future use during the:
    a. sous vide method
    b. cook-chill process
    c. sous-chill process
    d. chill-vide method

12. In a Chinese restaurant, the equipment star is the:
    a. griddle
    b. convection oven
    c. deep fryer
    d. wok

13. As additional items are placed in the oven, heating or cooking time may increase by _____ or more per item.
    a. 25%
    b. 50%
    c. 75%
    d. 90%

14. Probably the most prominent piece of equipment in the full-service kitchen is the:
    a. convection oven
    b. tilting skillet
    c. traditional range
    d. microwave

15. Because evaporative coolers have no need of compressors, they operate at approximately _____ of the cost of operating a refrigerated air-conditioning unit of similar cooling capacity.
    a. 10%
    b. 15%
    c. 20%
    d. 25%

16. If your restaurant operates with a profit margin of around 5%, you'll need about $9,000 worth of sales to earn _____.
    a. $400
    b. $450
    c. $600
    d. $650

17. The_____, whose surface has sections separately controlled for temperature, can cook different foods at different temperatures at the same time.
    a. sectionalized range
    b. convection oven
    c. sectionalized griddle
    d. combination steamer/oven

18. _____ can act as cooking pots; when filled with water, they can be used for quick-cooking vegetables, cooking hams or frankfurters, reheating foods, hard-boiling eggs, cooking macaroni or spaghetti, or holding canned or containerized foods.
    a. Deep-fat fryers
    b. Low temperature ovens
    c. Microwave ovens
    d. Electric fryers

19. The _____ is simply a tank holding heated water in which hot foods in pots or crocks are placed to keep food warm and to avoid cooking.
   a. tilting skillet
   b. bain marie
   c. boiler
   d. infrared cooking tank

20. A(n) _____ takes in outside dry air and pass it through loosely woven pads.
   a. evaporative cooler
   b. convection refrigerator
   c. forced-air convection oven
   d. low-temperature dishwasher

SHORT ANSWER QUESTIONS

1. What is the overall goal of kitchen planning?

2. Name three kitchen equipment categories.

3. What is the goal of a health inspection?

INTERNET EXERCISE

1. Search the internet for new trends in sustainable restaurant equipment. Are there any trends not mentioned in this chapter? Create a list of items you found to share with the class.

ACTIVITY

1. Using the concepts discussed in the chapter, create a simple diagram of a restaurant floor plan. Be sure to keep traffic flows within the kitchen to a minimum.

CHAPTER 6:
FOOD PURCHASING

INTRODUCTION

Successful foodservice operators establish standards of food quality that please the clientele served. They also establish a purchasing system that helps ensure that the food is purchased, stored, and accounted for so that theft, waste, and overproduction are minimized. Receiving and storage practices are spelled out. A *food-purchasing system* includes periodic review of current buying practices and customer preferences and a readiness to change any part of the system as necessary.

OBJECTIVES

After reading and studying this chapter, you should be able to:
- o Explain the importance of product specifications.
- o List and describe the steps for creating a purchasing system.
- o Identify factors to consider when establishing par stocks and reordering points.
- o Explain selection factors for purchasing meat, produce, canned goods, coffee, and other items.

CHAPTER OUTLINE
When setting up a food-purchasing system:
- o Establish standards for each food item used
- o Establish a system that minimizes effort and losses and maximizes control of theft.
- o Establish the amount of each item that should be on hand
- o Identify who will do the buying and who will keep the system in motion
- o Identify who will do the receiving, storage, and issuing of items.

Sustainable Purchasing
- o Restaurants are moving towards buying more locally
  - o Cuts down freight costs
  - o Strengthens regional economies
  - o Supports family farms
  - o Preserves the local landscape
  - o Fosters a sense of community
- o Does not mean that it is a sustainable product.
  - o Also involves food production methods that are healthy
  - o Do not harm the environment

Food-Purchasing System
- o Steps
  - o Determine the food standards required to serve the market
  - o Develop product specifications
  - o Gather product availability information
  - o Have alternate suppliers in mind
  - o Select a person to order and receive supplies
  - o Set up storage space for maximum utilization
  - o Establish the amount needed to be stocked (par stock) for each item
  - o Set up inventory control system
  - o Decide on optimal delivery size to reduce cost of delivery and handling
  - o Check all inventories for quality and quantity or weight
  - o Tie inventory control and cost control system together

Purchasing Cycle
- o Can be set up to roll along efficiently
  - o System that repeats itself day after day with minimal demands

Who sets up the System? Who operates it?
- o The manager in consultation with the chef decides on product specification, selects purveyors and has a figure in mind for par stock.
- o One person only should set up and operate the food purchasing system.

Food Quality Standards
- o Standards for food quality are set to serve a particular market
  - o Determined by the owner and chef/cook

Buying by Specification
- o Each operation needs a quality of food that fits its market
  - o Quality needed varies with the market and food item being produced

How much inventory?
- o Every food item has a shelf life
  - o Length of time it can be stored without appreciable loss in quality or weight
  - o Nearly every food that contains a large amount of water shrinks with storage
  - o Temptation is to buy a large quantity when a price reduction is available

Par Stock and Reorder Points
- o Based on quantity used, storage space available, and availability of the product
  - o Fast moving items require more stock
- o The operator with a fixed menu has an advantage in buying
  - o Preparation of entrées can be done in terms of prepared items (e.g., so many trays stored under refrigeration)

Par Stock Based on Pre-prepared Foods
- o Operator with a fixed menu has an advantage in buying.
- o Purchasing can be based on the par stock of pre-prepared and stored items

Mechanics of Ordering
- o Best way to place orders
  - o Opinions vary
- o Standing order
  - o Predetermined order that is filled regularly
- o Formal Purchasing order
  - o Purchase order form

Types of Purchasing
- o Most of the populated areas of the United States have food distributors.

Buying from full-line purveyors
- o Carry a large line of supplies
- o Offer more one-stop shopping
- o Saves time and simplifies billing

Co-op Buying
- o Supplies products at cost, plus enough of a markup to cover the cooperative's cost
- o Nonprofit
- o Lower cost than profit purveyors

Beware
- o Avoid aligning yourself with a supplier, who, in turn, has suppliers who are not certified by quality inspectors.
- o A visit to any small food processor soliciting your trade may pay for itself.

Buying Meat
- o Principal factors in meat buying are
  - o Cut of the meat: what part of the animal
  - o USDA grade: fat content, tenderness, and cost
  - o Style: carcass, wholesale cut, or ready-to-serve portion

Purchasing Meat
- o Beef, veal, pork and lamb are frequently used on menus.
  - o Save money by using lower meat grade when moist heat cooking method is used.
  - o Beef can be purchased as a side of beef.
  - o Many use selected cuts of meat
  - o Meat buyers use the Institutional Meat Purchase Specifications (IMPS) and the Meat Buyer's Guide published by the North American Meat Processors Association (NAMP)

Government inspection and grades of meat
- o Inspection has been mandatory since 1907
- o Inspection falls under the USDA Food Safety and Inspection Service (FSIS)
- o Quality grades: prime, choice, select, standard, and commercial

Buying and Receiving Meat
- o Steps
  - o Get a copy of the Meat Buyers Guide
  - o Determine exactly what meat the restaurant needs
  - o Request bids for purchase specifications
  - o Receiver should check the temperature of the meat
  - o Look for weight, count, and sizes

Buying Fresh Fruits and Vegetables
- o Guidelines
  - o Select freshly picked, mature items and use them as quickly as possible
  - o Handle them as little as possible
  - o Distinguish blemishes that affect appearance and those that affect quality
  - o Check on maturity
  - o Avoid those that are overripe or show decay
  - o Be conscious of size and count
  - o Know containers sizes and check contents
- o Green Dining Best Practices when sourcing product follow these:
  - o Go Organic
  - o Go Seasonal
  - o Buy imported produce with credentials: certified environmentally friendly.
  - o Reduce transport greenhouse gases.

USDA Wholesale Produce Grades
- o Standards
  - o U.S. Fancy: highly specialized produce
  - o U.S. No. 1: most widely used in trading
  - o U.S. Commercial: inferior to U.S. No. 1, but superior to U.S. No. 2.
  - o U.S. Combination: combines percentages of U.S. No. 1 and U.S. No. 2
  - o U.S. No. 2: lowest quality practical to ship
  - o U.S. No. 3: used for highly specialized products

Canned Fruits and Vegetables
- o Standards are the concern of the FDA
  - o Labeling of ingredients
- o Operators that frequently use canned items
  - o Perform can cutting tests usually in late fall
- o Less expensive products
  - o May turn out to be superior

TRUE OR FALSE QUESTIONS

On the following questions, answer whether the statement provided is true or false.

T　　F　　1.　During the process of *flash freezing*, fish are immersed in a liquid chemical that brings them to 100°F.

T　　F　　2.　Product specifications need only be reviewed, not reset, each time food is ordered.

T　　F　　3.　Restaurateurs are letting the menu drive business, and many change menus and prices four times a year.

T　　F　　4.　Nearly every food that contains a large amount of water that expands with storage.

T　　F　　5.　A co-op is a nonprofit institution that is able to provide restaurant food and supplies at lower cost than the profit-oriented purveyors.

T　　F　　6.　Par stock and reorder points are relatively fixed and are changed only as sales volume changes appreciably or as the menu changes.

T　　F　　7.　U.S. Fancy grade is the most widely used grade in trading produce from farm to market and indicates good/average quality.

T　　F　　8.　In independent restaurants, the responsibility for food purchasing usually rests with the cook.

T　　F　　9.　Quality standards and the standard of fill of container are concerns of the FDA.

T　　F　　10.　When it comes to the par stock for canned foods, the amount that is considered a safe inventory may be ordered only when the supply is down to a specified amount.

FILL IN THE BLANKS: KEY TERM REVIEW

On the following questions, fill in the blank with the most appropriate key term.

1.　The reasonable amount of a product to have on hand is called _____.

2.　A(n) _____ calls for a par stock and a reorder point for each food item.

3.　Written standards for food called _____ are set, preferably in writing, before a restaurant opens.

4.　Many restaurants use _____ of meat either fresh or frozen, that way they don't have to pay a butcher or devote space for butchering; they simply find it more efficient to order exactly what they want fresh or frozen.

5 _____ can be thought of as a subsystem within the total restaurant system, which once installed can be set in motion, and can repeat itself.

6. Meat buyers should use the _____ numbering system for meat items.

7. The _____ is a set of fruit and vegetable grade standards.

8. The *As Purchased (AP)* has a price spread for a(n) _____ that needs nothing more than cooking.

9. The *As Purchased (AP)* price for a(n) _____ such as a whole loin, which can be butchered into sirloin steaks, obviously coats less than a portion cut.

10. The stock points that indicate more product should be ordered are called_____.

11. _____ control—the amount of food to be ordered and stocked—can be built into the purchasing system by reference to past records.

12. The _____, published by the National Association of Meat Purveyors (NAMP), lists all the meat specifications and uses a numbering system for meat items.

13. Beef can be purchased as a(n) _____, which is half a cow that can then be butchered into the desired cuts.

MULTIPLE CHOICE QUESTIONS: CONCEPT REVIEW

On the following questions, circle the choice that best answers the question.

1. The grade _____ of meat is similar to prime, although the animal has been grain fed for 150 days, for medium 120 days, and low 90 days.
   a. Select
   b. Standard
   c. Choice
   d. Commercial

2. Restaurants with lower-priced menus are likely to:
   a. feature fruits that are out of season
   b. feature fruits that are in season
   c. feature more vegetables than fruits
   d. feature a lot of meat

3. Who is responsible for maintaining inspection services at principal shipping points and terminal markets?
    a. Customs
    b. Shippers
    c. USDA
    d. Receivers

4. The lowest grade of produce quality practical to ship is:
    a. U.S. No. 1
    b. U.S. No. 2
    c. U.S. No. 3
    d. U.S. No. 4

5. The _____ grade of meat, which is popular in supermarkets, is a low-cost item and is more healthful than higher-quality grades.
    a. Select
    b. Commercial
    c. Prime
    d. Standard

6. According to the National Restaurant Association's "What's Hot" survey, the number-one trend among chefs was buying _____.
    a. energy efficient kitchen equipment
    b. local produce
    c. canned food items
    d. frozen meats

7. The grade most widely used in trading produce from farm to market and indicates good/average quality is known as:
    a. U.S. No. 1
    b. U.S. No. 2
    c. U.S. No. 3
    d. U.S. No. 4

8. Operators who frequently use canned fruits or vegetables perform can-cutting tests, usually in the _____.
    a. fall
    b. spring
    c. summer
    d. winter

9. The system of Inspection for all meat sold in the US by USDA is?
    a. Voluntary
    b. Done at the stock yards
    c. Mandatory
    d. For beef only

10. Which of the following grades is used for the best meat product available?
   a. Select
   b. Prime
   c. Choice
   d. Commercial

11. Food storage in a restaurant is arranged purposely to facilitate _____.
   a. receiving
   b. issuing
   c. inventory control
   d. all of the above

12. A can-cutting test should determine the _____.
   a. unit cost
   b. strength of the container
   c. viscosity of the liquid
   d. full weight

13. _____ are established to determine when to order specific items.
   a. Food specifications
   b. Standardized stocks
   c. Par stocks
   d. Reorder points

14. Par stocks are:
   a. the reasonable amount of items to have on hand.
   b. stock points that indicate more items should be ordered.
   c. none of the above.
   d. a and b.

15. The length of time an item can be stored without appreciable loss in quality or weight is called _____.
   a. maintenance period
   b. freshness time
   c. shelf life
   d. safety period

16. The grade _____ of meat comes from older cattle and lacks tenderness.
   a. Select
   b. Standard
   c. Choice
   d. Commercial

17. In _____ buying, management agrees to supply products at cost plus enough of a markup to cover the cooperative's cost.
a. full-line purveyor
b. co-op buying
c. competition
d. wholesale club

18. The first step in putting together a purchasing system is to determine the _____.
a. suppliers
b. food standards
c. inventory
d. storage areas

19. Fresh meat should be stored at a temperature of _____.
a. 25°F to 30°F
b. 30°F to 35°F
c. 35°F to 40°F
d. 40°F to 45°F

20. The grade _____ of meat is similar to choice, but is less juicy and tender.
a. Select
b. Standard
c. Choice
d. Commercial

21. Grading of beef, veal, lamb and pork is?
a. Mandatory for wholesomeness
b. Recommended by law
c. Voluntary for quality
d. Done by the processor

SHORT ANSWER QUESTIONS

1. What are the steps in a food purchasing system?

2. What do full-line purveyors provide?

3. What are the characteristics of co-op buying?

4. What is the purpose of following a buying specification?
5. What are the guidelines for buying Fresh Fruits and Vegetables?

INTERNET EXERCISE

1. Go to the North American Meat Processors Association Web site. Summarize one article under the "Best Practices" section.

ACTIVITY

1. Using the information provided in the text, create a simple flow chart for a food-purchasing system.

CHAPTER 7:
BAR AND BEVERAGES

INTRODUCTION

Restaurant bar and beverage operations present operators with challenges and opportunities. The challenges begin with training or transferring a liquor license and operating with strict controls. Establishing and maintaining a program is not only critical to the restaurant's success, but is also socially responsible. Opportunities exist for creating exciting cocktails and for the combination of wine with food.

OBJECTIVES

After reading and studying this chapter, you should be able to:
- o Explain how to obtain an alcoholic beverage license.
- o Identify factors to consider when developing the design and layout of a bar.
- o List guidelines for suggesting wines to accompany menu items.
- o Identify a restaurant's legal liability regarding the sale of alcoholic beverages.
- o List ways in which bartenders and others can defraud the restaurant bar and beverage operation.

CHAPTER OUTLINE

Introduction
- o Beverages
  - o Account for 25–30% of total sales
  - o Sales yield more profit than food sales
  - o Production cost is less than in the kitchen
  - o Margins are greater

Alcoholic Beverage Licenses
- o Each state has a Department of Alcoholic Beverage Control with executive power to license and regulate the manufacture, importation and sales of all alcoholic beverages in the state.

Types of Alcoholic Beverage Licenses
- o Most common
  - o On-sale general
  - o Off-sale general
  - o On-sale beer and wine
  - o Off-sale beer and wine
  - o On-sale beer

How to Apply for a License
- o Two main kinds of alcoholic beverage licenses: general liquor and a beer and wine license.
- o Application process can be lengthy
  - o States have jurisdiction over the sale of alcohol
  - o Notices stating that a license has been applied for must be placed in the newspaper and posted in the restaurant window

Bar Layout and Design
- o A number of factors affect bar location and design
  - o Type of restaurant
  - o Overall design and layout of the restaurant
  - o Intended prominence of the bar
  - o Number of bartenders required to operate the bar and beverage service
  - o Volume of business expected
  - o Degree of self-sufficiency of the bar
  - o Electric and water supply
  - o Construction costs of providing electric and water supply
  - o Distance to the storeroom and the dispensing system
  - o Location of the beer kegs and cooling equipment

Front Bar, Back Bar, Under Bar
- o Front bar
- o Back bar
- o Under bar

Placement of a Bar within the Restaurant
- o Bar location
  - o Should be in a location with easy access
  - o To be a highlight, place near the entrance in prominent lighting
- o Seating
  - o Some provide comfortable seating so the customers can relax
  - o Seats placed close together encourage conversation

Beverages
- o Restaurants make a higher profit margin on beverages.

Cocktails
- o Style of mixed drink
  - o Mixture of distilled spirits, sugar, water, and bitters
  - o Has come to mean almost any mixed drink containing alcohol
    - o Usually contains one or more types of liquor and one or more mixes
- o Cocktail categories
  - o Short drinks: up to 3.5 ounces
  - o Tall drinks: up to 8.5 ounces

- o Factors of a good cocktail
  - o Balance of the ingredients
  - o Quality of the ingredients
  - o Skill of the bartender

Spirits
- o Whiskey
  - o Made from a liquid that has been fermented and distilled from grain
  - o Aged, often for long periods
  - o Whiskey from Scotland is called scotch
  - o Most whiskey is blended
- o Bourbon
  - o Now produced mainly from corn
  - o Aged up to six years in charred barrels

White Spirits
- o Most common
  - o Gin: popular foundation of many drinks (e.g., martini, gin and tonic, etc.)
  - o Vodka: made from several ingredients,
  - o Rum: dark or light in color
  - o Tequila: distilled from the agave tequilana
  - o Cognac: distilled from wine and only from the Cognac region of France.
  - o Brandy: distilled from wine

Nonalcoholic Beverages
- o Include
  - o Sodas and juices
  - o Nonalcoholic beers
  - o Dealcoholized wines
  - o Nonalcoholic cocktails (e.g., Shirley temple)
  - o Bottled waters
  - o Power drinks
  - o Coffee
  - o Tea

Bartenders
- o Top tasks
  - o Collect money for drinks served
  - o Check ID for legal age
  - o Balance cash receipts
  - o Avoid liability for intoxicated guests.
  - o Ensure clean glasses, utensils, and bar equipment
  - o Execute beverage orders from staff or guests
  - o Serve wine, sprits, cocktails and bottled or draft beer
  - o Clean bars, work areas, and tables
  - o Mix ingredients to prepare cocktails and other drinks.
  - o Serve snacks or food items to customers seated at the bar

Basic Bar Inventory
- o Selection depends on the type of restaurant
    - o Example: a trendy upscale restaurant will carry several premium brands
- o Sustainable bars
    - o New concept
    - o May include organic, "biodynamic," and/or local alcohol

Wines
- o Fermented juice of freshly gathered grapes
    - o Produced in temperate parts of the world
    - o First categorized by color: red, white, or rosé

Winemaking
- o Six steps
    - o Crushing
    - o Fermenting
    - o Racking
    - o Maturing
    - o Filtering
    - o Bottling
- o After fermentation
    - o Wine is transferred to racking containers
- o After maturing
    - o Wine is filtered
- o Wine is then clarified
    - o Adding egg white or bentonite removes impurities as it sinks to the bottom
- o Fine vintage wines
    - o Kept for a few years to further mature in the bottle and are consumed at their peak
- o White wines
    - o Mature quicker than red
    - o Often consumed within a few months of bottling

Sparkling Wines
- o Include: champagne, sparkling white wines, and sparkling rosé wines
    - o Sparkling comes from addition of carbon dioxide
- o Champagne
    - o Owes its sparkling quality to a second fermentation in the bottle

Fortified Wines
- o Include: sherries, ports, Madeiras, and marsalas
    - o They have brandy or wine alcohol added
    - o Sweeter than regular wine
    - o Each has several subgroups with a range of aromas and tastes

Aromatic Wines
- o Fortified and flavored with herbs, roots, flowers, and barks
    - o Can be sweet or dry
- o Known as aperitifs

o   Normally enjoyed before a meal to stimulate digestive juices

Wine Tasting
o   Wine tasting can enhance a restaurant's appeal and help guests enjoy and learn more about wines.

Wine Bottles and Glasses
o   Know wine bottles and glasses by their shapes
    o   Bordeaux
    o   Burgundy
    o   Champagne
    o   Mosel and Alsace
    o   Fortified Wines
o   Wine glasses are not only drinking tools-proper glasses you enjoy color, bouquet and taste.

How to Select a Wine List
o   How much budget and space available.
o   Wine selection should be appropriate for restaurant
    o   Naturally, an Italian restaurant will feature wines from Italy
o   Consider varietal type of grape and, most importantly, what's on the menu
    o   Pairing food with wine is critical to the enjoyment of the meal
o   Layout and format of the menu and wine list.

Wines with Food
o   Guidelines
    o   White wine: served with white meat—pork, turkey, chicken, veal, fish, and shellfish
    o   Red wine: served with red meat—beef, lamb, duck, and game
    o   Champagne: served throughout the meal
    o   Port and red wine: goes well with cheese
    o   Dessert wines: complement desserts and fresh fruits that are not highly acidic
    o   Dishes cooked in wine: best served with wines of that variety
    o   Regional food: best served with wine of the same region
    o   Wines are best not served with salads with vinegar dressings, chocolate, or strong curries

Responsible Alcoholic Beverage Service
o   Guidelines
    o   Write a responsible alcohol-serving mission statement outlining your position on drinking and safety
    o   Review local and state liquor laws
    o   Assess the operation's clientele
    o   Make a plan for developing and maintaining relationships with law enforcement officials and transportation organizations
    o   Establish a comprehensive program of ongoing staff training
    o   Create a schedule of management audits of policy and practice

     o   Create a system of actions that demonstrate support for responsible and enjoyable drinking
- Programs should include responsible actions
  - Example: a trained person at the door to Check IDs, etc.
- Encourage a "designated driver" program
- Provide taxi numbers to servers for use with intoxicated guests.
- Encourage food consumption
- Dramshop laws
  - Enacted by state legislators bring alcohol awareness training to the forefront.

Third Party Liability
- Owners, managers, bartenders, and servers
  - Liable if they serve alcohol to minors or intoxicated people
- Dramshop laws
  - Legislation that governs the sale of alcoholic beverages
- Combating underage drinking
  - Major brewery distributed a booklet showing the authentic design and layout of each state's driver's license
- Trade associations
  - Have produced a number of preventive measures and programs aimed at responsible alcohol beverage service

Controls
- Liquor inventory
  - Not properly controlled: can seriously affect the restaurant's bottom line
  - It is safe to assume, that given a chance, liquor will be stolen
  - Institute a weekly or biweekly audit

Controlling Losses
- Measures
  - Limit bar access to bartenders and make them accountable for pouring-cost results
  - Give incentive bonuses for good results
  - Require that drink orders be rung into the register before drinks are made
  - Use a remote system in which servers must ring up the order before it goes to the bartender
  - Install a surveillance camera
  - Install an alarm on the bar door
  - Do not allow bags brought into the bar area
  - Provide lockers in another area
  - If bartenders make mistakes, have them written off and signed for by management
  - Cushion bar floors to reduce breakage
  - Set up a system that allows employees to report incidents anonymously
  - Be careful in hiring employees: check references and do background check

Ways to Steal in a Restaurant or Bar
- Estimates

   o 25% of employees steal regardless of controls in place
   o 25% will not steal regardless of controls in place
   o 50% will steal if given the opportunity
 o Practitioners Publishing Company's Guide to Restaurants and Bars
   o 99 ways to steal in a restaurant or bar

Coffee and Tea
 o Coffee must fit the clientele
   o People tend to like the coffee with which they grew up
   o Widely traveled people
   o Coffee served in restaurants is a blend
 o General types
   o Robust, heavier flavored
   o Mountain grown, lighter, milder
 o Coffee vendors
   o Often supply the restaurant operator with a coffee-making machine
 o Tea and in particular, iced tea
   o Called the Champagne of the South

TRUE OR FALSE QUESTIONS
On the following questions, answer whether the statement provided is true or false.

T F 1. Today, a reasonable sales split is about 25% to 30% beverage sales and 70% to 75% food sales.

T F 2. Textures are the qualities in food and wine that we feel in the mouth, such as softness, smoothness, roundness, richness, thinness, creaminess, chewiness, oiliness, harshness, and so on.

T F 3. An on-sale general license authorizes the sale of all types of alcoholic beverages for consumption off the premises in original, sealed containers.

T F 4. The speed rack holds all of the top shelf liquor.

T F 5. In the food and beverage industry, it is estimated that 50% of employees steal regardless of the controls in place.

T F 6. Once an alcohol license is obtained, liquor may be purchased only from a wholesaler or manufacturer.

T F 7. To avoid or solve liquor control problems, owners should institute a daily audit.

T F 8. The legislation that governs the sale of alcoholic beverages is called dream stop litigation.

T   F   9.   Flavors are food and beverage elements perceived by the olfactory nerves as fruity, minty, herbal, nutty, cheesy, smoky, flowery, earthy, and so on.

T   F   10. For restaurants, there are three main kinds of alcoholic beverage licenses.

FILL IN THE BLANKS: KEY TERM REVIEW

On the following questions, fill in the blank with the most appropriate key term.

1.   By creating a convivial place for _____, restaurateurs can offer a place for relaxation, socialization, and entertainment.

2.   The bar setup is divided into three areas: the _____, _____, and _____.

3.   For restaurants, there are two main kinds of _____: a general liquor license and a beer and wine license.

4.   The main equipment in the under bar is the speed rack, which contains the _____ brand liquors.

5.   Once alcohol has been certified organic for three years, it can be considered _____.

6.   To avoid or solve liquor_____, institute a weekly or biweekly audit.

7.   Each state has a(n) _____, with the exclusive power, in accordance with laws enacted, to license and regulate the manufacture, importation, and sale of all alcoholic beverages in the state.

8.   The name and logo of the beer is usually displayed on a(n) _____, supplied by the distributor and located in view of the guests on the bar counter or, occasionally, on the back bar counter.

9.   The _____ is for aesthetics and functions as a storage and display area.

10. Most restaurants use the back bar to add atmosphere by displaying _____.

MULTIPLE CHOICE QUESTIONS: CONCEPT REVIEW
On the following questions, circle the choice that best answers the question.

1. In order for any sparkling wing to be called "Champagne" it must come from
    _____.
    a. Italy
    b. Portugal
    c. California
    d. France

2. Which of the following licenses authorizes the sale on the premises of all types of beer,
    wine, and malt liquor?
    a. Off-sale beer and wine
    b. On-sale general
    c. Off-sale general
    d. On-sale beer and wine

3. Where does one apply for a liquor license?
    a. ServSafe
    b. State liquor authority
    c. District Court House
    d. National Restaurant Association

4. The main equipment in the under bar is the _____.
    a. premium-brand liquors
    b. well brand liquors
    c. speed rack
    d. b and c

5. Wine is first categorized by _____.
    a. smell
    b. color
    c. region
    d. type (e.g., still, sparkling, fortified, etc.)

6. Red wine gains its color during which of the following processes?
    a. Crushing
    b. Racking
    c. Fermentation
    d. Filtering

7. Which of the following licenses authorizes the sale of all types of alcoholic beverages for
    consumption off the premises in original, sealed containers?
    a. Off-sale beer and wine
    b. On-sale general
    c. Off-sale general
    d. On-sale beer and wine

8. After maturing, the wine is filtered to help stabilize it and remove any solid particles still in the wine. This process is called _____.
   a. fining
   b. filtering
   c. fermentation
   d. racking

9. Sherries, Ports, Madeira's, and Marsala's are fortified wines, meaning they:
   a. are fermented for longer periods than any other type of wine
   b. are fermented for a shorter periods than any other type of wine
   c. are flavored with herbs, roots, flowers, and barks
   d. have brandy or wine alcohol added to them

10. The second step in the winemaking process is _____.
    a. crushing
    b. racking
    c. fermentation
    d. filtering

11. The better known red varietal wines include all but which of the following?
    a. Cabernet Sauvignon
    b. Zinfandel
    c. Merlot
    d. Pinot Noir

12. Which of the following licenses authorizes the sale of all types of alcoholic beverages—namely, beer, wine, and distilled spirits—for consumption on the premises?
    a. Off-sale beer and wine
    b. On-sale general
    c. Off-sale general
    d. On-sale beer

13. The Director of Alcoholic Beverage Control heads the department and is appointed by the _____.
    a. governor
    b. state attorney
    c. president
    d. superintendent

14. The current price of a license is _____.
    a. $10,000 to $15,000
    b. $20,000 to $25,000
    c. $30,000 to $35,000
    d. $40,000 to $45,000

15. Beverage sales yield _____.
    a. more profit than food sales
    b. less than profit food sales
    c. the same profit than food sales
    d. more production costs than food sales

16. Wine is _____ by adding either egg white or bentonite, which removes impurities as it sinks to the bottom of the vat.
    a. clarified
    b. fermented
    c. filtered
    d. fined

17. Notices stating that a license has been applied for must be placed in the newspaper and posted in the window of the restaurant. This notice must be posted for a minimum of _____.
    a. 14 days
    b. 21 days
    c. 30 days
    d. 60 days

18. A tall drink contains up to _____ ounces of liquid.
    a. 2.5 ounces
    b. 3.5 ounces
    c. 6.5 ounces
    d. 8.5 ounces

19. _____ is made from several different ingredients, predominantly barley, corn, wheat, rye, sugar beet molasses, and potatoes.
    a. Rum
    b. Whiskey
    c. Tequila
    d. Vodka

20. The typical margin on a fountain drink is about_____.
    a. 65%
    b. 75%
    c. 85%
    d. 95%

21. The best way to select coffee is to:
    a. inspect the beans for oil
    b. consult a coffee expert
    c. taste it yourself
    d. serve it to a taste panel of typical patrons

22. What is called "The Champagne of the South"?
    a. Chicory
    b. Bourbon
    c. Tea
    d. Whiskey

SHORT ANSWER QUESTIONS

1. List the six steps of the wine making process.

2. Briefly describe what happens during each of the steps you listed above?

3. What makes a wine "vintage"?

4. Name five main responsibilities of a bartender?

5. What should a bartender do if a guest suddenly appears intoxicated?

INTERNET EXERCISE

1. Search the Internet to find the alcoholic beverage licenses requirements of your state. Make a print out of your findings to share with the class.

ACTIVITY

1. Draw a bar layout using the information provided in the chapter. Be sure to include the back bar, under bar, and front bar, as well as the main components contained in each area.

CHAPTER 8:
OPERATIONS, BUDGETING, AND CONTROL

INTRODUCTION

Restaurant operations are divided into front and back of the house. The chef, to make a production schedule for the day based on the par levels required, the volume of business expected, and the estimated guest menu selection, uses standardized recipes. The chef monitors production and checks dishes as they leave the kitchen. Either the chef, or a manager is at the pass to ensure a smooth expedition of all plates. In the front of the house are an opening and a closing manager. The opening manager checks on the expected level of business—based on the prior year's business, the day's weather, and any other relevant factors. Stations are assigned to servers and a service meeting is held to inform everyone, of the specials and any training detail to focus on. Then they have a meal followed by action stations. The manager and servers ensure that the service goes well and that guests are delighted. Control of food and beverage items is critical to the overall success of the restaurant. This chapter describes inventory taking, the calculation of food- and beverage-cost percentages, and controllable expenses. Labor is the largest controllable cost, and examples are given to plan and monitor labor costs. Productivity analysis, operating ratios, and seat turnover are also discussed.

OBJECTIVES

After reading and studying this chapter, you should be able to:
- o Describe front-of-the-house operations.
- o Describe back-of-the-house operations.
- o Identify ways to control food, beverage, and labor costs.
- o Discuss methods of guest check control.

CHAPTER OUTLINE

Restaurant Operations
- o Split between back and front of the house
  - o Back of the house areas
  - o Front of the house

Front of the House
- o Refers to
  - o Hosts, bartenders, servers and bussers
  - o Opening and closing manager
- o Curbside appeal
  - o First impression

- o First thing restaurant managers do

- o Forecast how many guests are expected and share that information with the kitchen
- o Guest count
  - o Arrived at by taking the same day last year and factoring in things like today's weather, day of the week, etc.
- o Managers
  - o Make sure everything goes smoothly
  - o Goals are set for each key result area
  - o Schedules and checklists help organization

Back of the House
- o Sometimes called the "heart" of the operation
  - o Kitchen: center of production
  - o Production sheets: detail all tasks necessary to bring food quantities up to par stock and to complete preparation on time
    Chef: makes sure all menu items are prepared according to standardized recipes and the line is ready for service
    - o May act as a caller during service
- o Tips for restaurant managers by *Foodservice Where House*
  - o Manage costs effectively
  - o Increase sales
  - o Be consistent
  - o Deliver superior service
  - o Manage time wisely
  - o Create positive work environment
  - o Motivate the team
  - o Be a good example
  - o Reward as often as possible

Control
- o There is so much food and beverage in a restaurant
  - o Unless management and owners exert tight control, losses will occur
  - o Programs may be used

Calculating the Food Cost Percentage
- o Should be calculated at least monthly
  - o Formula: Cost/Sales × 100

Determining the Food Cost of a Particular Item on a Menu
- o FC%=EDC ÷ MP

Recycling to Reduce Costs
- o Recycling has become business as usual for 65% of restaurants

Liquor Control
- Critical to the success of the restaurant
- Management decides on the selling price and mark-up for beer, wine, and liquor
    - Sets the standard for beverage cost percentage

Controllable Expenses
- Various expenses that can be changed in the short term
    - Variable costs
    - Payroll
    - Direct operating expenses
    - Marketing
    - Heat, light, and power
    - Repairs and maintenance

Labor Costs
- May range
    - Depends on the type of restaurant and degree of service provided
- Projecting payroll costs
    - Requires preparation of staffing schedules and establishing wage rates
- Categories of payroll and related costs
    - Variable (percentage ratio to payroll)
    - Fixed (dollar amount per employee on the payroll)
- Variable items
    - Include those mandated by law
- Fixed items
    - Usually refer to employee benefits

Guest Check Control
- Without it a server can give food and beverages away or sell it
    - Guest checks can be altered and substitutions made if they are not numbered
- For tight control
    - Every check is audited, additions checked, and every check accounted for by number
- Some operators control income by having servers act as their own cashiers
    - Bring their own banks of $50 in change
    - Do not operate from a cash register but out of their own pockets
    - Deposit income in a night box at the bank

Productivity Analysis and Cost Control
- Various measures of productivity have been developed
    - Meals produced per employee per day, meals produced per employee per hour, etc.
- Simplest productivity measure
    - Sales generated per employee per year

TRUE OR FALSE QUESTIONS
On the following questions, answer whether the statement provided is true or false.

T   F   1.   The visual appeal of the building and parking area are important to potential guests.

T   F   2.   Restaurants can use programs like ChefTec, which shows the actual food cost compared with the ideal food cost.

T   F   3.   One of the more complicated employee productivity measures is sales generated per employee per year.

T   F   4.   Labor is the largest controllable cost.

T   F   5.   Variable cost items usually include things such as employee benefits and health insurance.

T   F   6.   Beverage inventory is done by "eyeball," measuring bottles of liquor in tenths.

T   F   7.   Combined, the beverage pouring cost should be 10% to 15% of beverage sales.

T   F   8.   Variable costs are normally controllable.

T   F   9.   Employee meals are treated as a taxable benefit by the IRS.

T   F   10.   For tight control, every guest check is audited, additions checked, and every check accounted for by number.

FILL IN THE BLANKS: KEY TERM REVIEW
On the following questions, fill in the blank with the most appropriate key term.

1.   _____ is the term used to describe the expenses that can be changed in the short term.

2.   In most full-service restaurants, the largest variable is _____.

3.   The hot plate area where plated items are passed to the food-servers is known as the ____ _____.

4.   The chef makes out a(n) _____ for each station, detailing all the tasks necessary to bring the food quantities up to par stock of prepared items and to complete the preparation on time.

5.   The _____ cycle begins with management deciding which brands to have for the well or house, then setting a par stock of beverages to have on hand.

6. In the _____ are the areas that include purchasing, receiving, storage, issuing, food preparation and service, dishwashing area, sanitation, accounting, budgeting, and control.

7. Goals are set for each _____. For example, sales goals include the number of guests per meal every day and the average check.

8. The selling price and mark-up for beer, wine, and liquor will set the standard for the _____.

9. _____ refers to the hosts, bartenders, servers, and bussers.

10. A(n) _____ is arrived at by taking the same day last year and factoring in things like today's weather, day of the week, and so on.

11. The _____ should be calculated at least monthly, by dividing the cost of food sold by food revenue.

12. _____ _____ must be in terms of what is appropriate for a particular style of restaurant: coffee shop, fast-food place, or dinner house.

MULTIPLE CHOICE QUESTIONS: CONCEPT REVIEW
On the following questions, circle the choice that best answers the question.

1. The normal pouring cost for beer is about _____.
   a. 10%
   b. 15%
   c. 20%
   d. 25%

2. Liquor pouring costs should be _____ percent of sales.
   a. 10% to15%
   b. 16% to 20%
   c. 25% to 30%
   d. 30% to 35%

3. In most full-service restaurants, the largest variable is _____.
   a. labor costs
   b. food costs
   c. beverage costs
   d. benefits

4. Who is at "the pass"?
   a. The chef
   b. The manager
   c. The server
   d. a or b

5. Several restaurants use the _____ to assist in managing the restaurant—it aids from planning to control.
    a. Red Book
    b. Blue Book
    c. Black Book
    d. Yellow Book

6. When using programs such as ChefTec, at the end of the day managers run a _____, which tells how many items were sold; multiply each menu item by the number sold, and that will give you what food should have cost for the day.
    a. forecasting report
    b. product mix
    c. production mix
    d. flash report

7. Which of the following lists the staff on both shifts of the day so you can easily see who's on duty?
    a. Prep sheet
    b. Lead sheet
    c. Production sheet
    d. Forecasting sheet

8. Ideally, the chef, having set the menu for the day checks inventory at the _____ to ensure sufficient food quantities.
    a. close the night before
    b. opening the day of
    c. beginning of the shift
    d. opening the day before

9. Which of the following details all the tasks necessary to bring the food quantities of prepared items up to par stock and to complete the preparation on time?
    a. Prep. sheet
    b. Lead sheet
    c. Production sheet
    d. Forecasting sheet

10. Restaurants can use programs like ChefTec, which shows the actual food cost compared with the ideal food cost. This is known as food _____.
    a. control
    b. mixing
    c. optimization
    d. planning

11. The first thing restaurant managers do at the beginning of a shift is to_____.
    a. assign server stations
    b. forecast how many guests are expected
    c. take inventory
    d. give a service meeting

12. Combined, the beverage pouring cost should be _____ of beverage sales.
    a. 10% to 20%
    b. 23% to 25%
    c. 35% to 30%
    d. 33% to 35%

13. Who is responsible for checking on the expected level of business—based on the prior year's business?
    a. Opening manager
    b. Closing manager
    c. Chef
    d. Servers

14. For a 30% cost, if a bottle of wine cost $10.00, the selling price is _____.
    a. $30.99
    b. $33.30
    c. $40.30
    d. $44.99

15. Taking the same day last year and factoring in things like today's weather, day of the week and so on, are all parts of arriving at a _____.
    a. yearly report
    b. semi-annual report
    c. guest count
    d. sales ratio

16. Salaries and wages (payroll) and related benefits; direct operating expenses, such as music and entertainment; marketing (including sales, advertising, public relations, and promotions); heat, light, and power; administration; and general repairs and maintenance are examples of _____ expenses.
    a. fixed
    b. controllable
    c. ratio
    d. depreciating

17. In terms of payroll, _____ items include those mandated by law: Social Security (FICA), unemployment insurance (state and federal), workers' compensation insurance, and state disability insurance.
    a. fixed
    b. controllable
    c. variable
    d. regulated

18. In terms of payroll, _____ items usually refer to employee benefits and include health insurance (an amount per employee per month), union welfare insurance (also an amount per employee per month), life insurance, and other employee benefits.
    a. fixed
    b. controllable
    c. variable
    d. regulated

19. A restaurant's profit is typically only _____ of total revenue.
    a. 2% to 6%
    b. 3% to 9%
    c. 11% to 13%
    d. 15% to 17%

20. The Energy Star program claims that if you follow their cost-effective recommendations, your investment in energy efficiency can give you up to a _____ return.
    a. 20%
    b. 30%
    c. 40%
    d. 50%

SHORT ANSWER QUESTIONS

1. Define controllable expenses.

2. Give five examples of controllable expenses.

3. What is the formula for food cost percentage?

4. What are the two categories that payroll costs fall into?

INTERNET EXERCISE

1.   Search the Internet for additional ways of controlling restaurant expenses that are not described in the chapter. Bring your findings to share with the class.

ACTIVITY

1.   If you were to hire a "shopper" to visit your restaurant, what type of things would you ask them to report on? Make of list of items to share with the class.

CHAPTER 9:
FOOD PRODUCTION AND SANITATION

INTRODUCTION

Our culinary heritage draws heavily on the cuisines of other countries, notably Italy, France, China, and to a lesser extent several other countries. The cuisines of Native Americans and African Americans also influenced our culinary heritage. French chefs dominated our culinary history.

For the purpose of this chapter, food production begins with receiving. Restaurateurs need to specify convenient delivery times; check everything, especially the most expensive items; weigh everything and check for freshness; check temperature; and ensure that what is delivered is what was ordered.

Restaurants, like hospitals and schools, are public places where people from many walks of life and backgrounds come together. Every person carries harmful microorganisms or viruses that can be transmitted by food or drink. The restaurant operator is necessarily engaged in preventing that transfer of pathogens, a relentless war in which hot water, heat, refrigeration, and chemicals are used.

OBJECTIVES

After reading and studying this chapter, you should be able to:
- o Discuss America's culinary heritage.
- o Explain the main elements in receiving and storing perishable and nonperishable items.
- o Describe the key points in food production.
- o Discuss the various types of food poisoning and how to avoid them.
- o Develop and maintain a food protection system.

CHAPTER OUTLINE

Our Culinary Heritage
- o American cooking
    - o Formed on a matrix of national cuisines
    - o Menus are the common denominator of restaurants

Native American Influence
- o Lasting, yet sometimes overlooked, influence on American cuisine today
    - o American Indians from the Eastern Woodlands
    - o Native Americans

- o **African American Influence**
- o Soul food
    - o Food traditionally prepared and eaten by African Americans of the Southern U.S.
    - o Can be trace back to Africa

Italian Influence
- o Italy has a rich culinary tradition
    - o Offers a variety of foods
- o Italians cultivated fine cuisine long before the French
    - o Their influences have much in common
    - o In the ancient period, wealthy Romans spent lavishly in time and money on food and drink

French Influence
- o Lexicon of cookery
    - o Reflects the French contribution to the culinary scene
- o Most experts rank French cookery near or at the top of various national cuisines

French Chefs Dominate Culinary History
- o Include
    - o Vatel (maitre d'hotel to the Prince de Conde)
    - o François Pierre de La Varenne
    - o Antoine Carême
    - o Felix Urbain-DuBois
    - o Georges August Escoffier
    - o Monseiur Boulanger

French Sauces and Seasonings
- o Sauces: hallmarks of the French cook
    - o Particularly those thickened with roux
- o Five "mother" or leading sauces
    - o Béchamel
    - o Velouté
    - o Espagnole
    - o Tomato
    - o Hollandaise
- o Younger French chefs have invented ways of avoiding calories while retaining flavor
    - o Fresh foods, lower fat, and the avoidance of roux-thickened sauces are being featured

Receiving
- o Smart restaurateurs arrange with suppliers for all deliveries to be delivered at times convenient to the restaurant
    - o Copy of the order should be available for the receiver
    - o Management should check and sign for all deliveries

Storage
- o Should be arranged for easy receiving, issuing, and inventory control
  - o Dry-goods storeroom: canned, packed, and bulk dry foods are stored according to usage
  - o Rotational system
- o Systems
  - o Last-in, first-out (LIFO) system
  - o First-in, first-out (FIFO) system
- o During a period of inflation
  - o Two costs could be quite different

Food Production
- o Kitchen manager, chef, or cook
  - o Begins the production process by determining the expected number of guests
- o Product mix: list of what was sold yesterday
  - o Every morning
    - o Chef or kitchen manager determines the amount of each menu item to prepare
- o Cooking line
  - o Most important part of the kitchen layout
  - o Kitchen is set up according to what is ordered most frequently

Production Procedures
- o Production in the kitchen
  - o Critical to the success of a restaurant
  - o Timing is vital
- o Production starts with mise-en-place
  - o Assembly of ingredients and equipment for the recipe
- o Creating production sheets
  - o Count the products on hand for each station
  - o Determine production levels
  - o Decide on amount of production required to reach the level for each recipe
  - o When calculations are completed, sheets are handed to cooks
- o Use of production sheets
  - o Critical in controlling how cooks use products
  - o When one deviates from the recipe

Staffing and Scheduling
- o Proper staffing
  - o Critical for successful running of a kitchen

Foodborne Illness
- o United States Public Health Service
  - o Identifies more than 40 diseases that can be transferred through food
  - o Foodborne illness: disease that is carried or transmitted to human beings by food
  - o Three types of hazards to safe food: biological, chemical, and physical

Biological Hazards-Bacteria
- o Highest number of biological food-borne illness is caused by bacteria
  - o Single-celled microorganisms that are capable of reproducing in about 20 minutes
- o Can cause illness in two ways
  - o Disease-causing bacteria (e.g., pathogens)
  - o Other bacteria discharge toxins that poison humans when food containing them is eaten
- o Pathogenic bacteria causes illness in humans through
  - o Intoxication : Example: botulism
  - o Infection : Example: salmonella
  - o Toxin-mediated infection: Example: E. coli

Causes of Food-borne Illness
- o High protein foods
  - o Responsible for most food-borne illnesses
- o Three disease-causing microorganisms most common in the United States:
  - o Staphylococcus aureus
  - o Salmonella
  - o Clostridium perfringem

Controlling or Destroying Bacteria
- o In order to grow, bacteria require
  - o Food, moisture, proper pH, and time
- o Potentially hazardous foods
  - o Those high in protein (e.g., meat, milk, and dairy products)

Bacteria and Temperature
- o Temperature
  - o Most important element for bacteria survival and growth
  - o Temperature danger zone: 40°F to 140°F
- o Destroying bacteria
  - o Heat
  - o Chemical sanitation

Viruses
- o Examples: Hepatitis A and Norwalk Virus
- o Do not require a hazardous food in order to survive
  - o Can survive on any food or surface
  - o Do not multiply
  - o Not as affected by heat or cold
- o Once a virus enters a body cell, it takes over
  - o Forcing the cell to assist in production of more viruses

Chemical Contaminants
- o Increased use of pesticides
  - o Has caused concern about chemical contamination of foods
- o Other types of chemical contamination

      o   Restaurant chemicals (e.g., detergents)
      o   Overuse of preservatives and nitrates
      o   Acidic reaction of foods with metal-lined containers
      o   Contamination of food with toxic metals

Hazard Analysis of Critical Control Points
  o   Presents methods for systematically ridding kitchens of pathogens
  o   Seven basic steps
      o   Identify hazards and assess severity and risks
      o   Determine critical control points in food preparation
      o   Determine critical control limits for each CCP
      o   Monitor CCPs and record data
      o   Take corrective action whenever monitoring indicates a CCL is exceeded
      o   Establish an effective record-keeping system to document the HACCP system
      o   Establish procedures to verify that the HACCP system is working

Common Food Safety Mistakes
  o   Key areas of common food safety risks in day-to-day food production

Time/temperature
  o   Keep cool foods below 40°F and hot foods above 140°F

Cross-contamination
  o   Most occurs in food preparation

Poor personal hygiene
  o   Wash hands

Approaches to Food Safety
  o   Overall responsibility for foodservice has been given to the FDA
      o   Provides a model ordinance that is the basis for most local health ordinances
  o   Public health license to operate a restaurant is required
      o   Health officer makes an inspection

Food Protection as a System
  o   The more sanitation practices built into a system
      o   The more likely they will be carried out
  o   McDonald's success
      o   Emphasis on the sanitation system
  o   Systematize sanitation practices
      o   Build them into the manager's daily schedule

TRUE OR FALSE QUESTIONS

On the following questions, answer whether the statement provided is true or false.

T   F   1.   Historically, the French cultivated fine cuisine long before the Italians.

T   F   2.   Cuisine Minceur is the "cuisine of thinness."

T   F   3.   When hot foods must be cooled, they should be chilled quickly in an ice bath or with running water.

T   F   4.   Fusion cuisine is a blending of the techniques and ingredients of two different cuisines – such as Japanese and French.

T   F   5.   In costing an inventory, the LIFO system costs the item at the price paid for the merchandise purchased last.

T   F   6.   When it comes to classic culinary terms, the vast majority are straight from the kitchens of Italy.

T   F   7.   The cooking line is the most important part of the kitchen layout.

T   F   8.   Production starts with mise-en-place.

T   F   9.   The product mix is a list of what was sold on the same day last year.

T   F   10. The Escoffier Cookbook became the bible for thousands of cooks for many years.

FILL IN THE BLANKS: KEY TERM REVIEW

On the following questions, fill in the blank with the most appropriate key term.

1.   French cuisine includes literally hundreds of sauces but basically there are five _____, each with a number of variations.

2.   _____ is a natural contaminant of meat and is commonly found in the intestinal tract of healthy humans.

3.   The disease-causing bacteria known as_____, feeds on nutrients in hazardous foods and, given favorable conditions, multiply rapidly.

4.   _____ is the blending of the techniques and ingredients of two different cuisines—such as Mediterranean and Chinese or Thai and Italian.

5.   The _____ may consist of a broiler station, window station, fry station, salad station, sauté station and desert station—just to name a few.

6. _____ is the assembly of ingredients and equipment for the recipe.

7. The _____ gives the quantity of each menu item to be prepared and increases the efficiency and productivity by eliminating guesswork.

8. Every morning the chef or kitchen manager determines the amount of each menu item to prepare and then _____ of those menu items in the refrigerators are checked.

9. _____ present a special problem because, in a favorable environment, they produce enterotoxins impervious to boiling water temperatures or the other temperatures commonly associated with food production.

10. In costing an inventory, _____system costs the item at the price paid for the merchandise purchased last and the _____ system uses the price actually paid for the item.

11. Unlike_____, which usually runs its course in a few days, infectious hepatitis has a   long incubation period.

12. As few as ten _____ germs in a salad can make healthy people ill.

13. Every morning the _____ determines the amount of each menu item to prepare.

14. Recently there was an outbreak of _____ in packages of spinach that were traced to one production facility in California.

15. Our _____ draws heavily on the cuisines of other countries, notably Italy, France, China, and to a lesser extent several other countries.

16. _____ cuisine was introduced as people became more health conscious.

17. _____ has a long incubation period, 10 to 50 days, before its symptoms of yellow discoloration, severe loss of appetite, weight loss, fever, and extreme tiredness set in.

18. _____ of food-borne or water-borne diseases are usually caused by unfiltered drinking water, shellfish from polluted waters, and, especially, poor personal hygiene.

19. _____, the best-known example of infection caused by bacteria, live in the intestines of chickens, ducks, mice, and rats.

20. Management interest in _____ and insistence on sanitation is the only practical way to protect employees and the public from diseases that are most certainly present when hundreds of people sit down to eat in a public restaurant.

MULTIPLE CHOICE QUESTIONS: CONCEPT REVIEW

On the following questions, circle the choice that best answers the question.

1. The temperature danger zone, between _____, is the range in which bacteria can thrive and multiply most rapidly.
   a. 20°F and 40°F
   b. 40°F and 140°F
   c. 120°F and 140°F
   d. 140°F and 160°F

2. Symptoms of staphylococcus appear in _____.
   a. 1 to 2 hours
   b. 2 to 6 hours
   c. 6 to 12 hours
   d. 24 hours

   High-protein foods are _____.
   a. as hazardous as other types of food
   b. responsible for most of food borne illness
   c. less hazardous than other types of food
   d. rarely responsible for food borne illness

4. Pefringens symptoms appear _____ after consumption.
   a. 2 to 3 hours
   b. 8 to 24 hours
   c. 24 to 36 hours
   d. 36 to 52 hours

5. Which of the following causes a majority of the tourist symptoms commonly experienced in developing nations?
   a. Salmonella
   b. Staph
   c. E.coli
   d. Ebola

6. Salmonella symptoms normally show up _____ after eating.
   a. 2 to 6 hours
   b. 1 to 3 hours
   c. 12 to 36 hours
   d. 42 to 56 hours

7. What chefs dominate culinary history?
   a. American
   b. Italian
   c. German
   d. French

8. Which of the following became the bible for thousands of cooks for many years?
   a. The Escoffier Cookbook
   b. The Joy of Cooking
   c. The Joy of Eating
   d. Moosewoods

9. Velvety smooth sauces made from either thickened veal, fish, or chicken stock are called:
   _____.
   a. Velouté
   b. Béchamel
   c. Espagnole
   d. Hollandaise

10. Salmonella presents no problem if suspect foods are heated to _____.
    a. 125°F
    b. 135°F
    c. 145°F
    d. 165°F

11. Working over foods, long cooking times, and the making of forced meats are all characteristics of _____.
    a. haute cuisine
    b. nouvelle cuisine
    c. sous-vide cuisine
    d. all the above

12. Salmonella symptoms normally last _____.
    a. a day or two
    b. 2 to 7 days
    c. 24 hours
    d. 2 to 6 hours

13. The blending of techniques and ingredients from different types of cuisine is known as_____.
    a. haute cuisine
    b. nouvelle cuisine
    c. sous-vide cuisine
    d. fusion cuisine

14. Symptoms of staphylococcus last _____.
    a. a day or two
    b. 2 to 7 days
    c. 24 hours
    d. 2 to 6 hours

15. Restaurants should hold foods at internal temperatures of at least _____.
    a. 70°F
    b. 90°F
    c. 120°F
    d. 140°F

16. Pumpkin, various types of beans, squash, peppers, blackberries, raspberries, and tomatoes were all introduced to settlers through the _____.
    a. Italians
    b. Native Americans
    c. French
    d. African Americans

17. Soul food is a term used for an ethnic cuisine, food traditionally prepared and eaten by the _____, residing in the Southern United States.
    a. Italians
    b. Native Americans
    c. African Americans
    d. French

18. _____, single-celled microorganisms that are capable of reproducing in about 20 minutes, cause the highest number of biological food-borne illness.
    a. Viruses
    b. Bacteria
    c. Mold
    d. Algae

19. Proper hand washing includes using water as hot as the hands can comfortably stand, using a brush for the fingernails, and rubbing the hands together using friction for _____.
    a. 10 seconds
    b. 20 seconds
    c. 30 seconds
    d. 60 seconds

20. _____ organisms are found in soil, water, and dust. Keeping hot foods hot, cold foods cold, and preventing cross-contamination controls this bacteria.
    a. Bacillus cereus
    b. Salmonella
    c. E.coli
    d. Ebola

SHORT ANSWER QUESTIONS

1. What does *mise-en-place* mean and what does it have to do with production?

2. What three areas are the most common food safety risks in day-to-day food production?

3. Besides pesticides, what are the four types of chemical contamination that can occur at any point along the food supply chain?

4. How do viruses survive and thrive?

INTERNET EXERCISE

1. Search the Internet for effective restaurant sanitation practices. Make a list of at least ten practices to share with the class.

ACTIVITY

1. Search the internet to find various dishes from you own personal heritage. Print out three recipes to share with the class.

CHAPTER 10:
RESTAURANT LEADERSHIP AND MANAGEMENT

INTRODUCTION

Restaurant corporations of excellence regard their employee resources as their most valuable asset and competitive advantage. Leadership begins with a vision, a mission, and goals. Leaders create a vision, develop goals, communicate and motivate, problem-solve, and make decisions. Any restaurant that wants to optimize its potential will have extensive employee input, into not only the vision and mission, but also how to achieve or exceed them. Operating a restaurant requires countless decisions every day. Most decisions are made quickly and easily, but some require more thought or information. Motivation refers to what makes people tick.

Performance standards form the heart of the job description. Conflict management is the application of strategies to settle opposing ideas, goals, and/or objectives in a positive manner. The EEOC provides guidance on dealing with discrimination and harassment issues. Alternative dispute resolution (ADR) is a term for problem-solving and grievance resolution.

OBJECTIVES

After reading and studying this chapter, you should be able to:
- o Describe the characteristics of effective leaders.
- o Discuss some important factors that must be considered when leading restaurant employees.
- o Know several important management concepts.
- o Discuss conflict management.
- o Describe the process of conflict resolution.

CHAPTER OUTLINE

Leading Employees
- o Employee resources are most valuable asset and competitive advantage.
- o We need to realize that leadership of employee resources is critical
  - o We don't manage our employees, we lead them
- o Being a leader is exciting
  - o There are challenges, opportunities, and rewards
- o In the hospitality industry
  - o Almost everything depends on the physical labor of many hourly (or nonmanagerial) workers
- o How well employees produce:
  - o Depends largely on how well they are led
- o Leadership
  - o Process by which a person with vision is able to influence the activities and outcomes of others

- Vision
  - Articulation of the mission in an appealing way that it vividly conveys the future
  - Instills a common purpose, self-esteem, and a sense of membership
- Mission statement
  - Describe the purpose of the organization, the value employees are expected to maintain
  - Declaration of major goals and how to attain them.

Leaders and Associates
- Restaurants are dependent on large numbers of people to fill low-wage entry-level jobs
  - Washing dishes, busing tables, hosting, etc.
- Another level of hourly worker is the skilled or semiskilled
  - Cashiers, bartenders, cooks, and servers

Characteristics of Leaders
- Traits of effective leaders
  - Drive
  - Desire to influence others
  - Honesty and moral character
  - Self-confidence
  - Intelligence
  - Relevant knowledge
  - Power
- Power: ability to influence others to behave in a particular way
  - Legitimate power: derived from an individual's position
  - Reward power: derived from rewards
  - Coercive power: derived from the ability to threaten negative outcomes
  - Expert power: derived from personal charisma and respect and/or admiration

The Nature of Leadership
- Getting people to work for you willing and to the best of their ability.
- Formal authority
  - The right to command, given by the organization
- Real authority
  - Conferred by subordinates
  - You have to earn the right to lead them
- Steps to establishing a foundation for leadership development
  - Commit to investing the time, resources, and money needed
  - Identify and communicate the differences between management skills and leadership abilities
  - Develop quantifiable measurements that support leadership skills
  - Make leadership skills a focus of management training
  - Implement ongoing programs that focus on leadership skills
  - Know that in the right culture, leaders can be found at entry level
  - Recognize, reward, and celebrate leaders for their passion, dedication, and results
- LBWA (leadership by walking around)

o Spending a significant part of your day talking to your employees, guests, and peers

Employee Input, and What's in It for Me?
o To optimize restaurant potential
o Have extensive employee input

Policies and Procedures
o Policies and procedures
o Necessary even for small restaurants
o Without them we all know chaos prevails
o "Ground rules" of how to "play the game"
o Employees will respect an operator who has policies and procedures in place
o Good planning makes for a smooth production

Management Topics
o Most texts outline the elements as planning, communicating, organizing, decision making, motivating, performance management, and control.

Planning
o Planning provides direction for the organization to go in order to be successful
o Process of setting goals and determining how best to accomplish them
o Strategic plans
o Devised to steer the organization towards its vision and mission

o Steps in planning process:
o Forecasting
o Determining where the organization is and where it wants to be
o Setting goals and strategies to achieve the goals
o Evaluating results

Forecasting
o Part of planning
o Aims to predict what will happen in the future
o Determine where the organization is
o Determine where the organization wants to be operationally

Goal Setting and Strategies
o Set for each key result area
o Guest satisfaction
o Guest loyalty
o Sales
o Labor costs
o Food and beverage costs
o Energy costs
o Direct operating expenses and so on

Organizing
- o Purpose is to get a job done efficiently and effectively by completing these tasks
    - o Divide work into specific jobs and departments
    - o Assign tasks and responsibilities
    - o Coordinate diverse organizational tasks
    - o Cluster jobs into units
    - o Establish relationships among individuals, groups, and departments
    - o Establish formal lines of authority
    - o Allocate and deploy organizational resources

Decision-Making
- o Decision-making process
    - o Identification and definition of problem
    - o Identification of decision criteria
    - o Allocation of weights to criteria
    - o Development of alternatives
    - o Selection of alternative
    - o Implementation of alternative
    - o Evaluation of decision effectiveness
- o Types of decisions
    - o Programmed decision
    - o Nonprogrammed decision

Communicating
- o Communication is important
    - o Imparts an impression of the restaurant to guests
- o Interpersonal communications
    - o Verbal, nonverbal, body language, and intonation
    - o Active listening: really hearing and understanding what is being said

Motivating
- o What makes people tick
    - o Needs, desires, fears and aspirations within people that make them behave as they do

Performance Management
- o Forms the heart of the job description
    - o Describe what's, how-tos, and how-wells of a job
- o Each performance standard has three things about each unit of the job
    - o What the employee is to do
    - o How well it is to be done
    - o To what extent it is to be done

Control
- o Keeping track of costs, inventory, percentages and other factors.

Restaurant Management Issues
- o There are many restaurant management issues.

Sexual Harassment
- o EEOC Title VII of the 1964 Civil Rights Act
  - o Guidelines on sexual harassment
- o Types of sexual harassment
  - o Quid pro quo
  - o Environmental sexual harassment
  - o Third-party sexual harassment
- o Guidelines
  - o Be familiar with the company's sexual harassment policy
  - o Educate employees how to recognize and report sexual harassment
  - o Investigate reported situations promptly
  - o When you witness sexual harassment, follow your policy and take appropriate action
  - o Provide follow-up after instances of sexual harassment
  - o Prevent it by being visible

Conflict Management
- o Application of strategies to settle opposing ideas, goals, and/or objectives
- o Steps
  - o Analyze what is at the conflict center
  - o Determine the strategy that will be used
  - o Start pre-negotiations
  - o Re-assess the situation
  - o Start the negotiation phase
  - o Implement negotiations

Conflict Resolution
- o Guiding principles
  - o Preserve dignity and respect
  - o Listen with empathy and be fully present and identify the issues
  - o Find a common ground without forcing change and agree on the issues
  - o Discuss solutions
  - o Honor diversity, including your own perspective
  - o Agree on the solutions and follow up

Alternative Dispute Resolution
- o Problem-solving and grievance resolution approaches
  - o Addresses employee relations and disputes outside the courtroom
- o Purpose
  - o Provide employers and employees with a fair and private forum to settle workplace disputes
- o ADR a process offers the following options
  - o Open door policy
  - o Third-party investigations
  - o Fact finding
  - o Peer review
  - o Mediation

o   Arbitration

TRUE OR FALSE QUESTIONS
On the following questions, answer whether the statement provided is true or false.

T   F   1. The hospitality industry is composed of 45% part-time, short-term people.

T   F   2. Coercive power is derived from an individual's control over rewards.

T   F   3. How well employees produce and serve depends largely on how well they are lead.

T   F   4. Planning is the foundation of all the other elements of management.

T   F   5. A person's drive shows that he or she is willing and able to exert exceptional effort to achieve a goal.

T   F   6. With an open door policy employees have the opportunity to meet with managers to discuss issues.

T   F   7. In the hospitality industry almost everything depends on the physical labor of many salary workers.

T   F   8. Motivation must come from within.

T   F   9. There are about 76,000 EEOC cases a year.

T   F   10. An example of goal setting would be for sales of $20,000 per week for the month of July.

FILL IN THE BLANKS: KEY TERM REVIEW
On the following questions, fill in the blank with the most appropriate key term.

1. _____ _____ occurs when both parties cooperate with each other and try to understand the other parties concerns, while also expressing their own.

2. _____ _____ is a term for problem-solving and grievance resolution approaches to address employee relations and disputes outside the courtroom.

3. With ___ _____, the conflict is avoided by both parties and neither party takes action to resolve it.

4. _____ results when there is a high concern for one's own interest or one's own group.

110

5. _____ create a vision, develop goals, communicate and motivate, problem-solve, and make decisions.

6. In the restaurant business we spend most of our time _____ with guests and associates.

7. _____ is the application of strategies to settle opposing ideas, goals, and/or objectives in a positive manner

8. If you are the only person in a group that holds a different viewpoint, you will probably end up conforming to the group and not speaking your opinion, known as _____ .

9. _____ is defined as a "difference, variety, or unlikeness."

10. _____ is a part of planning that aims to predict what will happen in the future.

11. _____ should be relevant to the mission, specific and clear, challenging yet achievable, made in collaboration with employees, and written down with the strategies and tactics of how to meet them.

12. _____ is accomplished by spending a significant part of your day talking to your employees, guests, and peers.

13. If your employees believe that you are always looking out for their best interest, they are more likely to believe in you, and look up to you as their _____ .

14. _____ refers to what makes people tick: the needs and desires and fears and aspirations within people that make them behave as they do.

15. The _____ describes the purpose of the organization and outlines the kinds of activities performed for guests.

16. A(n) _____ decision is one that rarely happens, so it is handled differently.

17. The purpose of _____ is to get a job done efficiently and effectively by completing several tasks.

18. To _____ is to give variety to something; to engage in varied operations; to distribute over a wide range of types or classes.

19. A(n) _____ decision relates to decisions that occur on a regular basis.

20. _____ consists of "unwelcome advances, requests for sexual favors, and other verbal or physical conduct of a sexual nature."

MULTIPLE CHOICE QUESTIONS: CONCEPT REVIEW
On the following questions, circle the choice that best answers the question.

1. If you were to ask any hospitality leader what his or her greatest challenge is, the likely answer would be _____.
   a. motivation
   b. organizing
   c. planning
   d. controlling

   _____ is the result of low concern for your own interests or the interest of your group, which produces a lose/win outcome. The opposing party is allowed to satisfy their interest, while one's own interests are neglected.
   a. Accommodation
   b. Collaboration
   c. Competition
   d. Compromise

3. In the _____ type of sexual harassment, submission to or rejection of a sexual favor is used as the basis for employment decisions regarding that employee.
   a. third-party
   b. environmental
   c. quid pro quo
   d. facilitated

4. The "S" in SWOT assessment stands for _____.
   a. sales
   b. strengths
   c. shares
   d. strategic

5. _____ results from high concern for one's own interest or one's own group interest accompanied by moderate to high interest for the other parties involved.
   a. Accommodation
   b. Collaboration
   c. Competition
   d. Compromise

6. There are _____ steps in the decision-making process.
   a. 3
   b. 5
   c. 8
   d. 10

7. Turnover rate for hourly workers in full-service operations is _____.
   a. 25%
   b. 50%
   c. 75%
   d. 100%

8. The first step in the planning process is _____.
   a. forecasting
   b. goal setting
   c. developing strategies
   d. evaluation

9. The last step in the planning process is _____.
   a. forecasting
   b. goal setting
   c. developing strategies
   d. evaluation

10. The "W" in SWOT assessment stands for _____.
   a. weekly
   b. weaknesses
   c. waiting
   d. wishes

11. _____ means that something is given in exchange for something else.
   a. Repudiation
   b. Retaliation
   c. Quid pro quo
   d. Arbitration

12. In _____ sexual harassment, comments or innuendos of a sexual nature or physical contact are considered a violation when they interfere with an employee's work performance or create an "intimidating, hostile, or offensive working environment."
   a. third-party
   b. environmental
   c. quid pro quo
   d. facilitated

13. The "T" in SWOT assessment stands for _____.
    a. tables
    b. trends
    c. threats
    d. timing

14. _____ sexual harassment involves a customer or client and an employee.
    a. Third-party
    b. Environmental
    c. Quid pro quo
    d. Facilitated

15. The first step in establishing a foundation for leadership development is to:
    a. implement ongoing programs that focus on leadership skills
    b. commit to investing the time, resources, and money needed
    c. develop quantifiable measurements that support leadership skills
    d. make leadership skills a focus of management training

16. _____ authority is conferred on your subordinates, and you have to earn the right to lead them.
    a. Real
    b. Coercive
    c. Reward
    d. Formal

17. _____ power is derived from an individual's personal charisma and the respect and/or admiration the individual inspires.
    a. Legitimate
    b. Reward
    c. Coercive
    d. Expert

18. _____ power is derived from an individual's ability to threaten negative outcomes.
    a. Legitimate
    b. Reward
    c. Coercive
    d. Expert

19. _____ power is derived from an individual's position in an organization.
    a. Legitimate
    b. Reward
    c. Coercive
    d. Expert

20. _____ power is derived from an individual's control over reward.
    a. Legitimate
    b. Reward
    c. Coercive
    d. Expert

SHORT ANSWER QUESTIONS

1. Describe the four primary sources of power.

2. Explain the seven steps to establishing a foundation for leadership development

3. List the steps involved in the planning process.

INTERNET EXERCISE

1. Search the Internet for various management styles. Summarize at least three styles t share with the class. Include the style that you would be most likely to follow and the sty you would be least likely to follow.

ACTIVITY

1. Create a diagram or chart of your choice using the characteristics of leaders described 1 the text. Be sure to place more emphasis on the traits you think are most important and les emphasis on the traits you think are least important.

CHAPTER 11:

ORGANIZATION, RECRUITING AND STAFFING

INTRODUCTION

Staffing the restaurant is extremely important, because effective screening not only selects the best employees but also screens out undesirable ones. Effective recruitment selects people with the most positive service spirit and professionalism. Compliance with existing employment legislation is a must. The human resource cycle begins with defining jobs and organizing the restaurant. A task is a related sequence of work and a job is a series of related tasks. Task and job analyses examine the details of the work performed and form the basis of the job description. The job specification identifies the qualifications and skills necessary to perform the job. The two main approaches to task and job analysis are bottom up, which is used when the organization already exists, and top down, which is used when opening new restaurants.

OBJECTIVES

After reading and studying this chapter, you should be able to:
- o   Describe the processes for creating job and task analyses.
- o   Describe the components of a job description, and list the guidelines for creating one.
- o   Identify legal issues surrounding hiring and employment.
- o   Determine the legality of potential interview questions.

CHAPTER OUTLINE

Job Descriptions
- o   Well organized restaurant has written job descriptions and specifications.
- o   Guidelines
    - o   Describe the job, not the person in the job
    - o   Do not describe in fine detail
    - o   Use short, simple, and to the point sentences
    - o   Explain technical jargon if used
    - o   Make the description detailed enough to include all aspects of the job
    - o   Include essential functions and outcomes expected

Job Specification
- o   Lists education and technical/conceptual skills a person needs to satisfactorily perform the job
    - o   Once the tasks are described a separate section of the job description form can be developed

The Job Instruction Sheet

o Task analysis can be converted into job instructions
  o Serve as a guide for new employees and as a quality assurance measure for the maintenance of work standards
o Comprise a list of the work steps
  o Arranged in sequential order if there is a natural cycle to the work

Organizing People and Jobs
o Every restaurant is organized so these restaurant functions are performed
  o Human resources management and supervision
  o Food and beverage purchasing
  o Receiving, storing, and issuing
  o Food preparation
  o Foodservice
  o Food cleaning; dish and utensil washing
  o Marketing/sales
  o Promotion, advertising, and public relations
  o Accounting and auditing
  o Bar service
o As restaurants grow, specialization of function becomes necessary.

Staffing the Restaurant
o Key words in finding the right people and preparing them to work successfully
  o Recruitment
  o Pre-employment testing
  o Interviewing
  o Selection
  o Employment
  o Placement
  o Orientation and training

Recruitment
o Process by which prospective employees are attracted to the restaurant
  o In order for a suitable applicant to be selected for employment
o Must be carried out in accordance to federal and state employment laws
o Must tell applicants hat they want to know
  o What the job is all about
  o Where are you
  o What hours
  o What qualifications
  o How to apply
  o Features of the job-such as wages and benefits

Preemployment Testing
o Must be valid and reliable
  o Valid test: measures what it is supposed to
  o Reliable test: shows the same results with repeated testing
o Range of tests to select from

o Examples: intelligence, aptitude, achievement tests.

Interviewing
o Seek to identify certain behavioral characteristics that may determine successful employment practices.
o The purpose of the interview is to
    o Gain sufficient information to determine the applicant is capable of doing the job
    o Give information about the company and the job
    o Ask appropriate, but leading questions

Ideal Employee Profiles
o Employees
    o Constitute a large part of the restaurant's ambiance, spirit, and efficiency
    o Must fit with the restaurant style
    o Outgoing personalities fit well in the front of the house
    o It is important to give employees a chance to succeed

Selection
o Determining eligibility and suitability of a perspective employee
    o How well they will do the job and fit in with the team
    o Personal appearance, grooming, and hygiene are important
o Purpose is to hire an employee that will be a team player and exceed expectations

Employment of Minors
o Teenagers, beginning at age 16, are excellent candidates for almost every restaurant job
    o From bussing dishwashing to cooking and order taking
    o Federal regulations control the work permissible for minors (under age 16)
    o Age restrictions state the maximum amount of hours a minor may work as well as the type of equipment they may work with or use.

Employment of Undocumented Aliens
o Immigration Reform and Control Act of 1986
    o Makes it illegal for employers to employ undocumented aliens
    o Several documents are used to determine the status of a prospective employee
    o Consequences of hiring undocumented aliens are substantial fines
    o The I-9 form is proof of having inspected the employees' documentation.

Employee Sources
o Include
    o Current employees via promotion
    o Restaurant website
    o Facebook, Twitter
    o Internet
    o State employment service
    o Schools
    o Vendors and customers

- o Youth groups, fraternities, and sororities
- o Walk-ins
- o Minority sources
- o Church groups
- o Veterans' organizations
- o Retiree organizations
- o TV, local cable
- o Community bulletin boards
- o Job fairs
- o Local partnerships

Civil Rights Laws
- o Equal Employment Opportunity (EEO)
  - o Recruitment, selection, and promotion practices which are open, competitive, and based on merit
- o American with Disabilities Act (ADA)
  - o Prohibits discrimination against employees who are disabled
  - o Requires making "readily achievable" modifications in work practices and conditions that enable them to work

Hiring People Who Are Physically or Mentally Challenged
- o Employees usually overlooked
  - o Those who are seriously disadvantaged emotionally, mentally, or physically
- o Keep in mind that you are selecting personnel for facilities used in the tasks to be performed
  - o Avoid hiring those at obvious risk for the work (e.g., a person with epilepsy may make a great book-keeper, but would be at risk as a cook)

AIDS
- o Acquired Immune Deficiency Syndrome
  - o Cannot be transmitted through the air, water, or food
  - o Contracted by Exchange of bodily fluids

Questions to Avoid: Application Form and during the Interview
- o Include
  - o Marital status
  - o Age
  - o National origin
  - o Family relationship
  - o Mental or physical handicap
  - o Race and/or sex
  - o Injured worker
  - o Religion

Questions You Can Ask
- o Include
    - o General opener
    - o Transportation
    - o Availability
    - o Hobbies/interests, Goals/ambitions
    - o Sports
    - o Languages
    - o Work experience
    - o Skill and Specific Job Related Questions, other interview Questions

The Multiple Interview Approach
- o Effective when there are plenty of applicants available
    - o During the first interview the candidate may be given a rating of 1 to 5

Telephone References
- o Follow up by phone
    - o More effective than a written request
    - o Direct the call towards applicants strengths and weaknesses
    - o Verify applicants' information
    - o Few people voluntarily make adverse comments about applicants

Careful Selection of Staff
- o Three main hiring objectives
    - o Hire people who project an image and attitude appropriate for your restaurant
    - o Hire people who will work with you rather than spend their time fighting your rules, procedures, and system
    - o Hire people whose personal and financial requirements are a good fit with the hours and positions you are hiring for

Screening out the Substance Abuser
- o Screen out the substance abuser
    - o Employment records may provide indicators

Pre-employment physicals and drug examinations
    - o Permissible as long as they pertain to the job and conform with ADA regulations

TRUE OR FALSE QUESTIONS
On the following questions, answer whether the statement provided is true or false.

T   F   1. Equal employment opportunity (EEO) is recruitment, selection, and promotion practices, which are open, competitive and based on merit.

T   F   2. Several leading restaurant chains have found that teenagers, beginning at age 13, are excellent candidates for most restaurant jobs.

T F 3. Task analysis can be converted into job instructions, which can serve not only as a guide to new employees but also as a quality assurance measure.

T F 4. The top down method is most frequently used when creating a task and/or job analysis in an organization that already exists.

T F 5. Acquired Immune Deficiency Syndrome (AIDS) cannot be transmitted through the air, water, or food.

T F 6. The bottom up method must be used when creating a task and/or job analysis in new restaurants because there are no existing employees to analyze.

T F 7. The National Restaurant Association spells out the work that may not be done by minors under 18 years of age.

T F 8. The Immigration Reform and Control Act of 1986 makes it legal for employers to employ undocumented aliens.

T F 9. The most useful source of employees is referrals by reliable present employees.

T F 10. One out of five Americans is considered disabled, according to the Census Bureau.

FILL IN THE BLANKS: KEY TERM REVIEW

On the following questions, fill in the blank with the most appropriate key term.

1. The _____ prohibits discrimination against employees who are disabled and requires making "readily achievable" modifications in work practices and working conditions that enable them to work.

2. _____ is the process of determining the eligibility and suitability of a prospective employee—not only how well a person can cook or serve, but also how he or she will fit in with the team.

3. A(n) _____ lists the education and technical/conceptual skills a person needs to satisfactorily perform the requirements of the job.

4. _____ is the process by which prospective employees are attracted to the restaurant in order that a suitable applicant may be selected for employment.

5. A(n) _____ is a related sequence of work.

6. Fundamental to the entire human resource function is _____ and _____, the in-detailed examination of the tasks and jobs to be performed.

7. Once the jobs are broken down into their various steps and the tasks are detailed, it is possible to develop _____ programs based on this information.

8. Many restaurants are considering or using _____ as a means of avoiding future personnel problems.

9. _____ seeks to identify certain behavioral characteristics that may determine successful employment practices.

10. _____ state that employers may not discriminate in employment on the basis of an individual's race, religion, color, sex, national origin, marital status, age, veteran status, family relationship, disabilities, or juvenile record that has been expunged.

11. The only medically documented ways in which _____ can be contracted are by exchange of bodily fluids, by shared needles, by infusion of contaminated blood, and through the placenta from mother to fetus.

12. The _____ was passed in 1967 to protect people over the age of 40 from discrimination.

13. The National Restaurant Association has formed a partnership with the _____ to promote their new Youth at Work Initiative.

14. The _____ makes it illegal for employers to employ undocumented aliens.

15. When tasks and job responsibilities are written down in organized form, they constitute a(n) _____.

MULTIPLE CHOICE QUESTIONS: CONCEPT REVIEW
On the following questions, circle the choice that best answers the question.

1. According to Brian Wilber, district manager of Bon Appétit Management Company, a chef is responsible for _____ of its food costs.
   a. 50%
   b. 75%
   c. 85%
   d. 95%

2. A person can be thought of as a clean-up person, but a better description would be "a person who expedites seat turnover." This is an example of emphasizing the _____.
   a. performance analysis
   b. qualifications
   c. job objective
   d. organization

3. The _____ of an employment test relates to whether it measures what it is supposed to measure and whether test scores predict successful job performance.
    a. reliability
    b. validity
    c. consistency
    d. objectivity

4. On school days, minors of what age may only work a maximum of 3 hours per day, 18 hours per week; on nonschool days, 8 hours per day, and 40 hours per week?
    a. 12 and 13
    b. 13 and 14
    c. 14 and 15
    d. 15 and 16

5. According to the Census Bureau ____ out of _____ employees are considered disabled.
    a. 1, 3
    b. 1, 4
    c. 1, 5
    d. 1, 6

6. A first interview may be given and the candidate rated from 1 to 5 on whatever factors are considered relevant to successful job performance. This is the _____ approach.
    a. public interview
    b. multiple interview
    c. single interview
    d. private interview

7. Which method of job analysis must be used in new restaurants because there are no existing employees to analyze?
    a. Bottom-up
    b. Top-up
    c. Bottom-down
    d. Top-down

8. A test is said to be _____ if essentially the same results are seen on repeated testing.
    a. valid
    b. objective
    c. reliable
    d. proactive

9. Several leading restaurant chains have found that teenagers, beginning at age _____, are excellent candidates for almost every restaurant job.
    a. 14
    b. 15
    c. 16
    d. 17

10. Minors of what age may not work before 7 a.m. or after 7 p.m. on school days; from June 1 through Labor Day, they may work until 9 p.m.?
    a. 12 and 13
    b. 13 and 14
    c. 14 and 15
    d. 15 and 16

11. The most useful source of employees is _____.
    a. referrals by present employees
    b. classified ads
    c. job fairs
    d. local partnerships

12. At age ___, teenagers may legally work at any job.
    a. 15
    b. 16
    c. 17
    d. 18

13. The _____ studies past sales experience records, confers with manager, keeps alert to holidays and special events, etc.
    a. Pantry Supervisor
    b. Server
    c. Assistant Manager
    d. Hostess/Host

14. Which of the following comprise a list of the work steps performed, arranged in sequential order if there is a natural cycle to the work?
    a. Task analysis
    b. Job instructions
    c. Job Analysis
    d. Job specification

15. When the organization already exists and the work behavior of the existing employees can be the basis for job analysis which approach would be used?
    a. Bottom-up
    b. Top-up
    c. Bottom-down
    d. Top-down

16. Only about _____ of all restaurants employ anyone with the title of chef.
    a. 1/4
    b. 1/3
    c. 2/3
    d. 3/4

17. _____ restaurants are more likely to have chefs than other restaurants.
   a. Quick-service
   b. Full-service
   c. Quick-casual
   d. Theme

18. There are no restrictions on working hours, even during school hours, at age _____.
   a. 13
   b. 14
   c. 15
   d. 16

19. The most effective way to check an employee's references is to follow-up by _____.
   a. written request
   b. phone
   c. e-mail
   d. fax

20. The Age Discrimination Act was passed in 1967 to protect people _____ from discrimination.
   a. under 16
   b. under 21
   c. over the age of 40
   d. over the age of 60

SHORT ANSWER QUESTIONS

1.   Discuss the three main hiring objectives in the text.

2.   What is the purpose of a job specification?

3.   What is the goal of a job interview?

4.   What happens during the process of selection?

INTERNET EXERCISE

1.   Search the Internet for several effective employment hiring practices. Make a list of practices not described in the chapter to share with the class.

ACTIVITY

1.   You are the assistant manager of a newly opening restaurant. The manager has requested that that you begin interviewing potential candidates for several serving positions. Create a list of questions that you would ask during the interviews to share with the class.

CHAPTER 12:
TRAINING AND SERVICE

INTRODUCTION

Restaurants often employ teenagers and young adults, many of them working part time and on their first job. Many or most do not expect to make a career in the restaurant field. Wages are low and employee turnover is high. For these and other reasons, training and management development is important. Training can be broken down into orientation training and job training. The purpose of training is to teach specific ways of doing things. Management development deals with principles and policies that managers use in relating to employees and customers. Guest relations is one of the aspects of restaurant keeping that makes it so interesting, and so frustrating. It is a continuous challenge, a challenge that is not for the timid, the tired, or the malcontent. The perfectionist and the thin-skinned cannot win at the customer relations game—there are too many variables. A sense of humor, good health, and a lively intelligence are decided assets. A desire to please and to serve is even more valuable.

OBJECTIVES

After reading and studying this chapter, you should be able to:
- o   List the goals of an orientation program.
- o   Compare and contrast behavior modeling and learner-controlled instruction.
- o   List guidelines for effective trainers.
- o   Describe characteristics of effective servers and greeters.
- o   Identify the seven commandments of customer service.
- o   List guidelines for handling customer complaints.

CHAPTER OUTLINE

Orientation
- o   Well-planned orientation programs
  - o   Help new employees become acquainted with the restaurant
    - o   Feel like they are a part of it
  - o   Most labor turnover occurs within the first few weeks of employment
    - o   Important to establish a bond between the employee and the restaurant
- o   Eight goals
  - o   Explain the company's history, philosophy, mission, goals, and objectives
  - o   Make the employee feel welcome
  - o   Let employees know why they have been selected
  - o   Ensure that the employee knows what to do and who to ask when unsure
  - o   Explain and show what is expected
  - o   Have employees explain and demonstrate each task
  - o   Explain various programs and social activities available

o   Show where everything is kept

Part-time Employees
o   Advantages
    o   No need to pay benefits
    o   Flexible schedule
o   Disadvantages
    o   Lack of continuity
    o   More need for training
    o   Less motivation

Training and Development
o   Objective: produce desired behavior
    o   Attitudes and skills for producing food and service that pleases the clientele
o   Employee development promotes
    o   Problem-solving abilities
    o   Analytical skills
    o   New perceptions
    o   New methodologies
o   Training produces skills quickly by breaking into segments and piecing them together into sequences.
o   Employee development programs
o   Deal with perspectives, attitudes and feelings about the restaurant, job, customers and boss
o   Planning for contingencies is part of development.
o   Problem solving can be programmed.

Training Programs
o   Training programs
    o   Most involve comprehensive step-by-step job learning
    o   Emphasize types of sales incentives
o   Efficient approach to training
    o   Analyze the job
    o   Break it down into the tasks performed
    o   Teach tasks in the sequence performed
o   Management decides how extensive written job instructions should be
    o   Being brief is an asset
    o   Guidelines for a job
o   Performance is evaluated on each shift.
o   Personnel training is the key to keeping satisfied, capable, confident and competent employees.

Training Aids
o   National Restaurant Association Educational Foundation (NRAEF)
    o   Developed informative training aids

Combine Training with Development

- o Every job calls for some training and some development.
- o Stay impersonal
- o Stay away from touch subjects.
- o Keep conversations brief and friendly

Slogans Help

- o "Thought packages" Example: Plan your work, work your plan.

Step-by-Step Training

- o Server training can be broken down and taught step by step
    - o Can also be summarized on a card small enough to be carried around in a pocket for easy reference

Training Theory

- o Proven guidelines
    - o All react to discipline and punishment.
    - o Reward (reinforce) desired learning.
    - o Reward or punish immediately after observed behavior.
    - o Spaced training is more effective than long period of training.
    - o Expect learning to proceed irregularly.
    - o Expect wide differences in the ability to learn.

Methods for Training Employees

- o Many ways to train employees as there are learning styles.

Behavior Modeling

- o Closely related to role playing, this technique depicts the right way to handle:
    - o Handle personnel problems
    - o Interview
    - o Evaluate applicants
    - o Make decisions
    - o Emphasis on interpersonal skills-*people handling*
- o Uses the innate inclination for people to observe others
    - o Discover how to do something new

Learner-controlled Instruction

- o Employees are given job standards to achieve
    - o Are asked to reach the standards at their own pace
- o Standards are set up for nearly everything that is done by a manager, who is expected to know about and be able to perform every task in the restaurant.

Manager as Coach

- o Trains and motivates
    - o Shows people how to perform
    - o Gives criticism when needed

- o Stresses the right way
- o Gives positive feedback
- o Triggers the will to win
- o Manage
  - o Implies purpose and mobilization of resources for given goals
  - o Graphic association is effective way to emphasize an idea.

Service
- o Guest service
  - o Important for all restaurants
  - o Guest relations is an aspect of marketing and sales
- o Psychology of foodservice
  - o Varies tremendously

Service Encounter
- o Many servers are skilled performers in the service encounter
  - o Server and guest are actors in a play
  - o Payoff for the guest: feeling of warmth, friendship, and ego enhancement
  - o Reward for the server: big tip and excitement of the drama

Service Personnel as a Family
- o Many managers do whatever they can to create a family feeling
  - o Encourage employees to eat and drink on the premises
  - o Reduce meal prices
  - o Sponsor employee parties

Greeters
- o First and last person a guest encounters
  - o Smiling, well-groomed, friendly person
  - o Greeters who know the restaurant
  - o Main part of the host's job

The Server as the Independent Businessperson
- o It is too easy to set servers up as private businesspersons
  - o Operating as an independent business on the premises leased for nothing
- o Fast-paced dining rooms
  - o Call for teamwork

Foodservice Teams
- o Some restaurants operate with servers working two to a team
  - o Most common: server/busser team
- o Team system
  - o Entire serving crew works as a team
  - o Major advantage: hot food is served hot

Hard Sell versus Soft Sell
- o Hard sell
  - o May result in the guest feeling pressured
- o Soft sell
  - o Low key complete service
- o Clientele determines the best approach
  - o Service includes a number of other factors

Seven Commandments of Customer Service
- o Include
  - o Tell the truth
  - o Bend the rules
  - o Listen actively, almost aggressively
  - o Put pen to paper
  - o Master the moments of truth
  - o Be a fantastic fixer
  - o Never underestimate the value of a thank you

Formality or Informality
- o Depends on the kind of experience you are trying to deliver
  - o Some restaurants thrive on informality
  - o Others may be more formal

Setting the Table
- o Tables should be pleasing and inviting
  - o Cutlery and glassware should be spotless
  - o Once complete, setting should be pleasing to the eye

Taking the Order
- o Servers introduce themselves and take suggest beverages
  - o Main point: get the guest to make a selection from a variety of choices
- o Server may also describe food specials
  - o Then depart to obtain the beverage
- o Food orders
  - o Senior female order is taken first
  - o Ordered by seat number
  - o Beverages: served and cleared from the right-hand side and to a tray
  - o Some restaurants clear plates as soon as a person is done eating

Greeter or Traffic Cop
- o Greeter: host welcoming arriving guests
  - o First representative to interact with visitors
- o Rookie greeters
  - o First few weeks: outgoing, warm, and friendly

Magic Phrases
- o May include
    - o Welcome back
    - o We're happy you're here
    - o It's good to see you again
    - o I hope you like it/enjoy it
    - o May I take your plate?
    - o How was your evening?
    - o Sorry to have kept you waiting
    - o I'm sorry: I'll put that right.
    - o Have a nice trip home

The Difficult Guest
- o Once in a while, the server is confronted by a difficult guest
    - o Majority of handling complaints: falls into employee hands

Strategies for Handling Complaints
- o Win-win action tips
    - o Act immediately on a complaint
    - o Let the guest know you care
    - o Calm the guest, acknowledge problem, encourage feedback
    - o Tell how the problem will be addressed
    - o Invite the guest to express their feelings
    - o Never invalidate or make the guest wrong
    - o Offer appropriate and reasonable amends
    - o Nurture the relationship
- o Other tips
    - o Be diplomatic
    - o Remain calm, listen, and empathize
    - o Control your voice
    - o Get the facts
    - o Take care of the problem immediately
    - o If you take back an entrée, offer to keep the other meals warm in the kitchen

Tact: Always
- o Guests want common courtesy
    - o Recognition
    - o Respect
    - o A friendly welcome
- o Principal reason people dine out

TRUE OR FALSE QUESTIONS

On the following questions, answer whether the statement provided is true or false.

T   F   1. Experience has shown that the most practical and immediately beneficial way of training restaurant employees is the learner-controlled instruction method.

T   F   2. Most training programs involve comprehensible step-by-step job learning that utilize job checklists and differing styles of management control.

T   F   3. The Foodservice Management Professional Credential (FMP) has minimum requirements and a certification examination with five sections that must be passed before the certification is awarded.

T   F   4. Surprise quizzes and examinations are good ways to ensure performance at a high level.

T   F   5. Using part-time workers results in giving less training.

T   F   6. It should be expected that there will be periods during the training when no observable progress is made.

T   F   7. Many believe the learner-controlled instruction method is less costly than classroom instruction and reflects employees' different levels of motivation, energy, and ability.

T   F   8. A "piece of the action" is the term used by some restaurants in encouraging unit managers to acquire, through purchase, a percentage of the store they manage.

T   F   9. The restaurant has an obligation to provide employees with the skills necessary to perform the job.

T   F   10. The Bureau of Labor Statistics reports that well under half of all persons employed in foodservice occupations work part time.

FILL IN THE BLANKS: KEY TERM REVIEW

On the following questions, fill in the blank with the most appropriate key term.

1. _____ development deals with principles and policies that managers use in relating to employees and customers.

2. A well-planned _____ program helps new employees become acquainted with the restaurant and feel a part of it.

3. The objective in _____ _____ _____ employees is to produce desired behavior—attitudes and skills appropriate for producing food and service that pleases the restaurant's clientele.

4. Closely related to role-playing, which has been around a long time, _____ is a technique that depicts the right way to handle personnel problems, shows how to interview and evaluate applicants, and demonstrates decision-making.

5. The _____ model views restaurant managers as coaches, they are engaged in informal training much of the time—showing, telling, correcting, praising, and providing direction.

6. Employee _____ promotes problem-solving ability and provides analytical skills, new perceptions, and methodologies.

7. _____ transforms problems into challenges, excites the imagination, calls on pride, develops a sense of accomplishment and achievement, and provides opportunities to overcome obstacles.

8. _____ provides learning material that can be studied and learned by individuals at their own pace.

9. Many servers are skilled performers in the _____. The dinner house, and especially the lounge, is the stage.

10. Once in a while, the server is confronted by a(n) _____ who is determined to prove his manhood or vent her hostility on other customers, the serving personnel, or the manager personally.

11. Service personnel must be aware of the degree of _____ desired by their customers.

12. Servers should get down to eye level and make _____ with their guests.

13. Servers must be willing to participate in a(n) _____ effort. They have to be willing to contribute to the guest's satisfaction, whether or not they are in their section.

14. When low-key, complete service is expected, servers should go with a(n) _____ approach to selling.

15. When tables are plentiful, the question could be, "Would you prefer a table or a booth?" This is an example of _____.

16. Some restaurants thrive on _____, the servers may appear in tennis shoes and blue jeans, saying "Hi, I'm Bob, I'll be your server tonight."

17. "Will you have dessert?" This is one example of a(n) _____ sell.

MULTIPLE CHOICE QUESTIONS: CONCEPT REVIEW

On the following questions, circle the choice that best answers the question.

1. Tipping in New York City is probably higher than in most American cities, close to
    _____.
    a. 10%
    b. 15%
    c. 20%
    d. 25%

2. The 2009 State of Training and Development in the Hospitality Industry Report contains
    answers to _____ related questions.
    a. selection
    b. budget
    c. profit sharing
    d. location

3. Behavior modification is based on _____.
    a. college population studies
    b. studies on restaurant guests
    c. animal studies
    d. learner controlled instruction

4. The first goal for an orientation program is to:
    a. explain and show what is expected of employees
    b. ensure that employees know what to do and who to ask when unsure
    c. explain the company history, philosophy, mission, goals, and objectives
    d. explain profit sharing incentives

5. To be effective, learner-controlled instruction presumes the availability of _____.
    a. learning resources
    b. rewards
    c. customers
    d. coaches

6. The Foodservice Management Professional Credential exam covers _____ areas.
    a. three
    b. four
    c. five
    d. six

7. Psychologists tell us that inserting constructive criticism between two _____ softens
    the criticism while at the same time working the criticism.
    a. neutral statements
    b. negative statements
    c. behavioral rewards

d. favorable comments

8. Closely related to role playing, which has been around a long time, which of the following is a technique that depicts the right way to handle personnel problems, shows how to interview and evaluate applicants, and demonstrates decision making?
a. Behavior modeling
b. Awareness training
c. Learner controlled instruction
d. Coaching

9. The Bureau of Labor Statistic reports that:
a. well over half of all persons employed in the foodservice occupations work part time
b. in the quick service segment, the proportion of part-timers is lower
c. less than half of all persons employed in the foodservice industry work part time
d. in the fine dining segment, the proportion of part-timers is higher

10. The Educational Foundation of the National Restaurant Association has developed informational video tapes and CD-ROMs. Topics areas include all of the following except:
a. Alcohol awareness training
b. Back-of-the-house-training
c. Wine training
d. Profit sharing

11. The word "manage" implies _____.
a. purpose
b. development
c. punishment
d. criticism

12. Which of the following is a program in which employees are given job standards to achieve and asked to reach the standards at their own pace?
a. Behavior modeling
b. Awareness training
c. Learner controlled instruction
d. Carrot-and-stick method

13. Which of the following is a false statement?
a. The trainer should have written task instructions before beginning to teach and should list the key points around which instructions are built
b. After a task is learned, ask trainees for suggestions on how to improve the task
c. The best way to handle an overconfident trainee is to call them out in front of others
d. The trainer should learn what the employee already knows about the job before starting to train

14. Typically the tip percentage averages from _____ in other American cities.
    a. 10% to 15%
    b. 15% to 20%
    c. 20% to 25%
    d. 25% to 30%

15. Behavior modification theory urges:
    a. an immediate reward for whatever behavior is desired
    b. an immediate punishment for undesirable behavior
    c. that rewards may have negative effects
    d. insincere positive reinforcement

16. The Lettuce Entertainment training program lasts _____ days, for 8 hours daily.
    a. 3
    b. 4
    c. 5
    d. 6

17. Which method of training does T.G.I. Friday's use?
    a. Equity theory
    b. Step-by-step
    c. Carrot-and-stick
    d. Learner-controlled instruction

18. Which training method allows the learning to be absorbed and avoids fatigue?
    a. Long period of training
    b. Continuous training
    c. Spaced training
    d. Skipped training

19. Servers in which type of restaurant are seldom tipped?
    a. Family
    b. Theme
    c. Quick-service
    d. Casual

20. Much of labor turnover occurs within the first few _____ of employment.
    a. hours
    b. days
    c. weeks
    d. months

21. The food order should be taken by _____.
    a. asking the senior female for her order first
    b. asking the female that looks most ready for her order first
    c. starting from left to right
    d. starting from right to left

22. What is the first thing severs should do upon approaching a new table?
    a. Suggest beverages
    b. Give the specials
    c. Introduce themselves
    d. Take a drink order

23. What is the "hands-in-the-pocket" policy?
    a. No matter how obnoxious a patron becomes, never consider being physical in handling the situation.
    b. Servers should keep their hands in their pockets when not taking an order.
    c. Bussers and servers should always immediately put extra tips in their pockets when given to them from a guest.
    d. Always try to extract the biggest tip possible from guests.

24. Who is known as the as the creator of eggs Benedict, veal Oscar, and for aiding in the popularization of Thousand Island dressing?
    a. Charlie Trotter
    b. Julia Childs
    c. John Walker
    d. Oscar of the Waldorf

SHORT ANSWER QUESTIONS

1. Why is it important to have a well-planned orientation program?

2. Describe the benefits and the drawbacks of hiring part-time employees.

3. What is the main objective in training and development?

4. Name the three techniques used to train new employees.

5. What are the characteristics of a good server?

6. What is the main responsibility of the host/hostess?

INTERNET EXERCISE

1. Search the Internet for various training techniques and theories. Make a list of at least five effective training techniques and another list of five ineffective training techniques to share with the class.

2. Search the Internet for restaurant situations involving difficult guests. How were these situations handled? Make a list of the situations you find to share with the class. Have a discussion on how it could have been handled differently.

ACTIVITY

1. This chapter discusses several characteristics of effective managers. List ten characteristics that you think are the most critical to share with the class. Be sure to put them in order of importance.

CHAPTER 13:
TECHNOLOGY IN THE RESTAURANT INDUSTRY

INTRODUCTION

This chapter reviews the technology and its applications for front- and back-of-the-house restaurant operations. POS systems and various software programs are discussed. Most restaurants divide their technology into two parts: back and front of the house. Many systems integrate these so that operators can input and draw on the information from both programs. *Back-of-the-house*, or *back-office*, restaurant technology consists of product management systems for purchasing, managing inventories, menu management, controlling labor and other costs, tip reporting, food and beverage cost percentages, human resources, and financial reporting. Back-office systems aid inventory control by quickly recording the inventory and easily allowing new stock to be added. Calculations are done rapidly and monetary tools are given for each item, plus a cumulative total. Front-of-the-house technology revolves around the point-of-sale system and wireless handheld devices. *Point-of-sale* (POS) systems are the combination of hardware and software used is any business setting where transactions occur. While the most basic POS systems used in retail businesses function predominately as an electronic cash register, more dynamic and multifunctional versions are commonly used in hospitality businesses.

OBJECTIVES

After reading and studying this chapter, you should be able to:
- o Identify the main types of restaurant industry technologies.
- o List and describe the main types of software programs.
- o Identify factors to consider when choosing technology for a restaurant.

CHAPTER OUTLINE

Technology in the Restaurant Industry
- o Technology
    - o Has come a long way from mom-and-pop operators and their cigar box
    - o Independent operators may not require (or be able to afford) technology that chain operators are using

Back-of-the-House Technology
- o Consists of product management systems for
    - o Purchasing and managing inventories
    - o Menu management, Financial reporting
    - o Controlling labor and other costs
    - o Tip reporting, Human resources
    - o Food and beverage cost percentages

Purchasing and Inventory Control
- o Product management
  - o Tracks products through each inventory cycle

Inventory control
- o Systems quickly record inventory

Kitchen Display Systems (KDS)
- o Manage and control kitchen efficiency
  - o Provide highly visible, real-time information
  - o Installed in more upscale restaurants
  - o Fully integrated with point-of-sale (POS) systems
  - o Mounted in kitchen or food prep area

Food Costing
- o Personal digital assistant (PDA)
  - o Used to enter inventory amounts into the system
- o Bar code scanning
  - o Speeds up inventory-taking process
  - o Data is entered into the system, variance report is generated, and any significant variances are investigated
- o ChefTec & ChefTec Plus software
  - o Integrate programs

Menu Management
- o Link between food costing and menu management
  - o Menu management systems are food service programs used to manage front-of-house and back-of- house operations.

- o MenuLink
  - o Evaluates managers' produce purchasing
  - o Compares actual to expected food usage
  - o Tests proposed recipes and pricing changes

Labor Management
- o Interfaces back- and front-of-the-house
  - o Working hours
  - o Human resources information
- o Includes
  - o Application monitoring, recruitment, personnel information, I-9 status, tax status, availability, vacation information, benefit information, and scheduling

Financial Reporting
- o Front- and back-of- the-house systems
  - o May interface by transferring data to and from the central server
  - o Makes it easier to monitor

E-learning
- o Computer based training
    - o Delivered via the Internet or proprietary Internet sites
- o PeopleSoft
    - o Employees an access benefits and other information
- o The National Restaurant Association Educational Foundation
    - o Several online courses

Front-of-the-House Technology
- o Revolves around
    - o Point-of-sale (POS) systems
    - o Wireless handheld devices
- o New technologies
    - o Multimedia lobby displays
    - o Self-service kiosks
    - o Wireless payment-processing units
    - o In-store dashboard displays

POS Systems
- o Combination of hardware and software, where transactions occur.
- o Purposes include:
    - o Input of food and beverage orders
    - o Electronic cashier transactions
    - o Tracking of sales and payroll
- o POS system a standard component of operational costs
- o Advantages of POS systems include:
    - o Elimination of arithmetic errors
    - o Improved guest check control
    - o Increased average guest check
    - o Faster reaction to trends
    - o Reduced labor cost
    - o Reduced late charges

Selecting a POS System
- o Performance
- o User-interface designs

Table Management
- o Table management software
    - o Meticulous control of restaurant efficiency, consistency, and accuracy
    - o Example: MICROS Systems, Inc.

Pay at the Table
- o Handheld device may be provided to guests to
    - o Verify their bill
    - o Swipe their card

- o Include any tip
- o Print the receipt
- o Benefits to guests
  - o Peace of mind concerning security issues
  - o Ability to leave the restaurant a little sooner

PCI DSS

- o Payment Card Industry Data Security Standard established in order to reduce the risk of payment card fraud and prevent misuse of cardholder information.

POS Systems

- o Suppliers
  - o IBM: Linux servers and Sure POS 700 series
  - o Sharp: UP-5900 system
  - o NCR: 7454 POS Workstation, Real POS 70, and Comprise
  - o Micros: Eclipse PC Workstation

Mobile Phone Technology

- o It is essential to own a smartphone device of some type.
- o The various elements of a business's life cycle are continuously being influenced by mobile phone technology.
  - o Advertising and awareness
  - o Brand recognition and purchasing decisions
  - o Post-purchase behavior
  - o Loyalty
  - o Eventually dictates the entire consumer purchase process.
- o Mobile payment
- o Text messaging is used to communication throughout the hospitality industry.

Web-based Enterprise Portals

- o Offer centralization of applications
  - o Sales reporting
  - o Cash management
  - o In-store profit and loss statements
  - o Labor and food costs
  - o Prep
  - o Ordering
  - o Task lists
  - o POS data

Gift Card and Loyalty Programs

- o Customer relationship management (CRM)
  - o Deliver a 360-degree view of the guest's activities
  - o Gift cards are help increase revenue
  - o Final result: a positive return on investment.

Guest Services and Websites
- o Restaurant technology has evolved
  - o Restaurant can store and recall guests' preferences
  - o Additional advances

Restaurant Management Alert Systems
- o MICROS Alert Manager
  - o Monitors conditions and compares them to established standards
  - o New integration with the RES products and the on-premise paging
  - o Communications solutions made available by JTECH
- o Push-for-service
  - o System that a hotel or restaurant with remote areas can use to be notified by guests when they need to order food or beverage items.
- o Table locator systems
  - o Fast casual restaurants

TRUE OR FALSE QUESTIONS
On the following questions, answer whether the statement provided is true or false.

T F 1. When calculating the food and beverage cost percentage, a hand-held device called a PDA can enter the inventory amounts into the system.

T F 2. ChefTec and ChefTec Plus software solutions integrate programs with recipe and menu costing, inventory control, and nutritional analysis capabilities.

T F 3. There is a definite link between food costing and menu management.

T F 4. Labor management systems only interface back-of-the-house employee working hours.

T F 5. The point-of-sale terminal is the workhorse of restaurant operations.

T F 6. POS systems are continuing to increase in price.

T F 7. Aloha's virtual order processing communicates between the kitchen and wait staff.

T F 8. Restaurant Web sites need an appealing, user-friendly design and functionality, including accessibility and interactivity.

T F 9. Computer-based training is decreasing in the workplace.

T F 10. Most restaurants divide their technology into two parts: back- and front-of-the-house.

FILL IN THE BLANKS: KEY TERM REVIEW

On the following questions, fill in the blank with the most appropriate key term.

1. Among the many operations, _____ technology consists of product management systems for purchasing, managing inventories, menu management, controlling labor and other costs.

2. When calculating the food and beverage cost percentage, a hand-held device, called a _____, can enter the inventory amounts into the system.

3. _____ include a module to monitor applications, tax forms, vacations, benefit information, and scheduling based on the forecasted volume of business for each meal period.

4. The _____ terminal is the workhorse of restaurant operations.

5. MenuLinks _____ function is used to determine what offers work best, so that coupon building may be directed toward those items.

6. Computer-based training, known as _____, is delivered via the Internet or proprietary Internet sites.

7. _____ provide highly visible, real-time information to manage and control kitchen efficiency.

8. Through easy-to-use automation, _____ systems allow the restaurant to effortlessly handle time-sensitive guest demands associated with reservations and waiting times.

9. With _____ _____ _____, all of the activities are tracked and controlled from a central database, allowing restaurant operators to recognize their guests with the most frequent spending patterns

10. _____ _____ can be described as the transaction between the producer and consumer of a good or service, which allows the consumers to pay for their purchase directly from their phone.

MULTIPLE CHOICE QUESTIONS: CONCEPT REVIEW

On the following questions, circle the choice that best answers the question.

1. Back of-the-house, or back-office, restaurant technology mainly consists of:
    a. product management systems for purchasing, managing inventories, and controlling labor, and other costs
    b. the point-of-sale (POS) system
    c. guest service
    d. wireless handheld devices

2. Back-office systems aid inventory control by quickly recording the inventory and easily allowing new stock to be added. This is called _____.
   a. food costing
   b. purchasing
   c. inventory control
   d. labor management

3. The handheld device used to enter inventory amounts into the system is called a:
   a. PDA.
   b. LAN.
   c. POS.
   d. SQL.

4. MenuLink's menu management function is used to _____.
   a. determine offers for couponing
   b. take inventory
   c. make schedules
   d. determine liquor costs

5. Which of the following is the workhorse of restaurant operations?
   a. PDA
   b. LAN
   c. POS
   d. SQL

6. Which of the following concentrates on restaurant performance improvements allowing the restaurant operator to identify areas in which to increase revenues, improve operational efficiency, and improve guest service?
   a. MCO
   b. HFE
   c. EEG
   d. SQL

7. Darden Restaurants recently introduced a _____ software system that employees use to access benefits and other information through its intranet site.
   a. ServSafe
   b. PeopleSoft
   c. Bar Code
   d. MenuLink

8. Technological improvements have made it possible to do a restaurant's food cost percentage in about _____ of the time it used to take and with more accuracy.
   a. one-quarter
   b. half
   c. one-third
   d. three-quarters

9. When a restaurant's employees are not productive and customer-service levels are not up to snuff, such problems can often be traced to the design of the _____ interface, ranging from complicated screen layouts to inappropriately sized buttons and the poor use of colors for different menu items.
   a. PDA
   b. POS
   c. HFE
   d. SQL

10. All front-of-the-house employees should take a _____ course.
    a. responsible alcohol service
    b. food safety
    c. menu design
    d. time management

11. About _____ of Fortune 1000 companies have significant e-learning initiatives underway.
    a. 65%
    b. 75%
    c. 85%
    d. 95%

12. Easy access to restaurant Web sites is important. It is also helpful to include:
    a. staff photos and names
    b. staff names and contact information
    c. the managers personal contact number
    d. directions and parking information

13. When calculating the food and beverage cost percentage, using a hand-held device to enter the inventory amounts into the system is called _____.
    a. food costing
    b. purchasing
    c. inventory control
    d. labor control

14. NCR offers a Human Factors engineering team to:
    a. provide quantitative data for evaluating current store performance levels and user interface designs
    b. create couponing systems
    c. create restaurant Web sites
    d. critique menu recipes and offer suggestions for improvement

15. Back-office systems aid inventory control by:
    a. offering self-service kiosks that allow guests to interact and ease host stand congestion.
    b. providing visible, real-time information to manage and control kitchen efficiency.
    c. generating and sending coupons to guests.
    d. quickly recording the inventory and easily allowing new stock to be added.

16. Front-of-the-house technology revolves around the _____.
    a. PDA
    b. LAN
    c. POS
    d. SQL

17. The Federal Trade Commission's Consumer *Fraud and Identity Theft Complaint Data* report stated that _____ was the most common form of reported identity theft.
    a. social security number fraud
    b. credit card fraud
    c. driver's license theft
    d. character identity theft

18.   The primary competency of an Internet portal is the _____.
    a. storing of guest preferences
    b. coupon offerings
    c. guest ratings
    d. centralization of applications

19. MICROS _____ allows operations to manage by exception by monitors conditions and comparing them to established standards.
    a. Compris
    b. Alert Manager
    c. Table Service
    d. Real POS

20. All back-of-the-house employees should take the _____courses offered by the National Restaurant Association Educational Foundation.
    a. Bar Code
    b. ServSafe
    c. PeopleSoft
    d. TimePro

SHORT ANSWER QUESTIONS

1. TimePro from Commeg Systems has a time, attendance, and scheduling feature. What is the purpose of this feature?

2. What do labor management systems include?

3. What does Cambridge Investments use MenuLink for?

4. MenuLink has developed a new feature for its Back Office Assistant called the Automated Raw Material Transfer. What does this feature perform?

INTERNET EXERCISE

1.   Search the Internet to find additional restaurant technologies that were not discussed in the chapter. Make a list of at least five technologies to share with the class.

ACTVITY

1.   Using one of the technologies in the text, create a flow diagram illustrating how it facilitates the transfer of information throughout the restaurant to support operations.

CHAPTER 14:
RESTAURANT BUSINESS AND MARKETING PLANS

INTRODUCTION

No restaurant can reach its potential without an understanding of the principles of a good business plan and marketing. Some streetwise owner-managers do not possess formal marketing skills; however, their informal skills are often as savvy as those of any marketing expert. Marketing focuses on the needs and wants of guests, whereas sales, focuses on the needs and wants of the restaurant operator. Once the potential market is identified, planning can take place. The business and marketing plan is completed after an assessment of the marketplace, the competition, and the restaurant's strengths, weakness, threats, and opportunities. The marketing plan, if properly completed and executed, will greatly assist in ensuring that the restaurant's goals are met. The main components of the marketing plan are known as the four Ps: product, place, promotion, and price.

OBJECTIVES

After reading and studying this chapter, you should be able to:
- o Describe the various forms of business ownership
- o Discuss the advantages and disadvantages of each form of business.
- o Identify the major elements of a business plan.
- o Develop a restaurant business plan.
- o Conduct a market assessment.
- o Discuss the importance of the four Ps of the marketing mix.
- o Describe some promotional ideas for a restaurant.

CHAPTER OUTLINE

Introduction
- o Business plans
  - o Increase probability of success
- o Restaurants
  - o Are experiencing extreme challenges
- o New restaurant operation has a choice of legal entities
  - o Sole proprietorships
  - o Partnerships
  - o S corporations

What Business Entity is Best?
- o All businesses are operated as proprietorships, partnerships or corporations.
  - o The choice of entity affects: Taxes, liability, legal relationships, business entity.

Sole Proprietorship
- o Simplest and the most prevalent
  - o Restaurant operator does not draw a salary for federal income tax purposes
  - o Proprietor is not an employee
- o Advantages
  - o Simple and reasonable salary
  - o Funds can be withdrawn
  - o Business can be discontinued or sold
- o Disadvantages
  - o Owner cannot participate in qualified pension and/or profit sharing plans
  - o Owner is liable for everything
  - o No legal existence apart from the owner(s)

Partnership
- o Any venture where two or more persons endeavor to make a profit
  - o General partnerships
  - o Limited partnerships
- o Advantages
  - o Flexible
  - o No double taxation
  - o Choice of limited or general partnership
- o Disadvantages
  - o Same problems of legal liability as sole proprietorship
  - o Partner may create debts for the partnership
  - o Difficult to divide assets if business fails
  - o Death, disagreement, and/or ill health can make perfection into a nightmare
  - o In bad times partners always see the other as at fault

Restaurant as a Corporation
- o Legal entity similar to a person
  - o Can borrow, buy, conduct business and must pay state and federal taxes on profits
- o Deciding whether to incorporate
  - o Often depends on insurance coverage
- o Advantages
  - o Limited liability
  - o Ease of availability and affordability of insurance through group plans
  - o Corporate fringe benefits are available
  - o Can sell and distribute stock
  - o Investor friendly
- o Disadvantages
  - o Double taxation
  - o Takes a lot of money to set up
  - o Usually requires legal and accounting advice
  - o Can lose control if too much stock is distributed

S Corporation
- o Permits business entity to operate as a corporation
  - o Allows it to avoid paying corporation taxes
  - o Avoids a double tax upon liquidation
  - o Useful for a family restaurant
  - o Ideal if owners do not want to accumulate after-tax income or if shareholders are in a low tax bracket
- o Provides tax advantages for dependent children or parents
- o Corporation taxes are avoided
  - o Profits from restaurant are taxed according to income brackets
  - o IRS requires officers draw a fair salary so company earnings are not overstated
- o Benefits over two percent of annual salary cannot be deducted

Buy–Sell Agreement with Partners
- o Preserves continuity of ownership in the business upon sale
  - o Made up of several legal clauses that can control business decisions

Legal Aspects of Doing Business
- o Steps required in California
  - o Form a business entity
  - o Identify necessary permits and licenses
  - o Identify local restrictions on proposed business licenses
  - o Obtain environmental or similar permit as needed
  - o Obtain state sales tax permit
  - o Determine applicability of employer registrations
  - o Get insurance
  - o Comply with relevant statutes and regulations with respect to employee's wages
  - o Fulfill occupational and health requirements
  - o Assess applicability of antidiscrimination laws
  - o Check for eligibility for government assistance
  - o File fictitious business name
  - o Meet posting requirements
  - o Obtain and return tax return filings
  - o Learn reporting and notice procedures in event of employee injury

State Registration
- o Plans to open a new business should be discussed with the secretary of state's office.
  - o Fees run about $100 for registering a new business.
  - o Most states have income tax on wages
  - o State Department of Employee Compensation must be contacted.
  - o Cities require permit to operate a business

Sales Tax
- o New business is registered with the state revenue
  - o Most states require an advanced deposit or bond

The Patient Protection and Affordable Health Care Act (PPACQ), and other Regulations
- o Most important topic affecting restaurants
  - o Larger restaurant chains are affected more than small independent restaurants.
  - o Cost implications
  - o Many unanswered questions
  - o Fewer full time employees
- o Restaurants and hotels may also have to deal with other regulations and laws:
  - o Paid sick leave requirements
  - o Nutrition labeling requirements
  - o Smoking laws
  - o Depreciation of restaurant improvements
  - o Drink taxes
  - o Special event permits

Business Plan
- o Improve chances of operational success
  - o Assist in obtaining financing
  - o Communicate to potential investors
  - o Define operational purposes
- o Key ingredient
  - o Sustainability
- o Elements
  - o Cover sheet
  - o Description of the business
  - o Description of concept, licensee, and lease
  - o Market analysis and strategy
  - o Competitive analysis
  - o Pricing strategy
  - o Advertising and promotional campaign
  - o Other information
  - o Financial data
  - o Existing restaurant balance sheet
  - o Appendices
- o Mission statements
  - o Generally do not change
- o Goals
  - o Reviewed as often as necessary
  - o Established for each key operational area
- o Strategies or action plans
  - o Who is going to do what, when, and in what order
  - o Specific dates
- o Marketing Philosophy
  - o Patterns the way to relate to guests, employees, purveyors, and the general public
  - o Finding out what guests want and providing it at a fair price
  - o Asks would-be operators, who what when

The Difference Between Marketing and Sales
- o Marketing
  - o Broad concept
  - o Includes sales and merchandising
  - o Determines who will patronize the restaurant and what they want in it
  - o Ongoing effort
  - o Gets into psyche of present and potential patrons
  - o About solving guest problems
- o Sales
  - o Part of marketing
  - o Focuses on seller needs
  - o Activities that stimulate the patron to want what the restaurant offers
  - o Sales mentality exists when seller thinks about only of his or her needs
  - o Closely related to advertising, promotion, and public relations

Marketing Planning and Strategy
- o Marketing plans
  - o Must have realistic goals while leaving a reasonable profit margin
- o SWOT analysis
  - o Strengths, weaknesses, opportunities, and threats

Market Assessment and Market Demand
- o Market assessment
  - o Analyzes community, potential guests, and competition
  - o Helps to answer the all-important questions: need and who is guest?
- o Market demand factors
  - o Population in the catchment area
  - o Demographic split of this population

Market Potential
- o Estimated maximum total sales revenue of all suppliers of a product in a market during a certain period
  - o How many people in the market area are potential customers?
  - o What is the potential for breakfast, for lunch, for dinner?
  - o Will your restaurant attract guests from outside the immediate market area?
  - o Who is your market?

Market Segmentation, Target Market, and Positioning
- o Market
  - o Total of actual and potential guests
  - o Generally segmented into groups of buyers
  - o Within these groups are target markets
- o Three Typical Segmentations
  - o Geographic: Country, state/province, county, city, and neighborhood
  - o Demographic: Age, sex, family life cycle, income, occupation, education, religion, and race

- o Behavior: Occasions, benefits sought, user status, usage rates, loyalty status, and buyer readiness
- o Positioning
  - o Once the target market is identified
  - o Key to positioning: perception

Competition Analysis
- o Analyzing competition's strengths and weaknesses
  - o Helps formulate marketing goals and strategies to use in the marketing action plan
- o Comparison benefit matrix
  - o Shows how your restaurant compares to the competition

Marketing Mix: The Four Ps
- o Every marketing plan must have realistic goals
  - o While leaving a reasonable profit margin
- o Cornerstones of marketing
  - o Place (location)
  - o Product
  - o Price
  - o Promotion

Place/Location
- o One of the most crucial factors in a restaurant's success
- o Ingredients for success
  - o Good visibility
  - o Easy access
  - o Convenience
  - o Curbside appeal and parking

Product
- o Main ingredient: excellent food
  - o People will always seek out excellent food
- o Three levels of restaurant product
  - o Core product: function part for the customer
  - o Formal product: tangible part of product
  - o Augmented product: other services
- o Product analysis
  - o Covers quality, pricing, and service

Atmospherics
- o Design used to create a special atmosphere
  - o Experiencing greater emphasis

Product development
- o Innovative menu items
  - o Added to maintain or boost sales

Product positioning
- o Conveys the best face/image of the restaurant
    - o What people like most about it
    - o How it stands out from the competition

Restaurant differentiation
- o Owners usually want their restaurant to be different in one or more ways
    - o Call attention to food or ambiance

Product life cycle
- o Introduction to decline

Price
- o Revenue-generating variable in the marketing mix
- o Important consideration in the selection of a restaurant.
- o In restaurant marketing, several factors affect price:
    - o Relationship between demand and supply
    - o Shrinking guest loyalty
    - o Sales mix
    - o Competitions' prices
    - o Overhead costs
    - o The psychological aspect of price setting
    - o Need for profit

Cost-based pricing
- o Calculates cost of ingredients
    - o Multiplies by a factor of three to obtain a food cost percentage of 33

Competitive pricing
- o Checks competition to see what they are charging for the same item
    - o Choose other item or alter the ingredients

Contribution Pricing
- o Method of computing a product's selling price so that the price contributes to the gross income.
- o Amount of labor cost involved with the preparation and service of the menu item
    - o Relationship of demand and supply
    - o Declining guest loyalty has an effect on pricing
    - o The price-value relationship is extremely important
    - o Sales mix is an important aspect in setting pricing levels

Price and Quality
- o Direct correlation between price and quality

Promotion
- o Goals of a promotional campaign
    - o Increase consumer awareness
    - o Improve consumer perceptions
    - o Entice first-time buyers
    - o Gain higher percentage of repeat guests
    - o Create brand loyalty
    - o Increase the average check
    - o Increase sales (particular meal or time of day)
    - o Introduce new menu items
- o Promotions are conducted to increase sales in several ways:
    - o Increase guest awareness of the restaurant or menu
    - o Introduce new menu items
    - o Increase customer traffic
    - o Increase existing guests' spending
    - o Increase demand during slow periods

Advertising
- o Extent to which a restaurant needs to advertise depends on several variables.

In-house advertising
- o Vacant space be used for advertising media
    - o Bathroom stalls, paper cups, movie tie-ins

Filling in the Periods of Low Demand
- o Tie-ins and two-for-ones
- o Loss-leader meals

Advertising appeals
- o Six benefit appeals used in restaurant advertising:
    - o Food quality
    - o Service
    - o Menu variety
    - o Price
    - o Atmosphere
    - o Convenience

Social Media
- o Potential for attracting customers
    - o Twitter
    - o Facebook
    - o Pinterest
    - o Tumblr
    - o Instagram

Travel Guides for Free Advertising
- o Listing can be worth thousands of dollars in extra sales
  - o Mobil Travel guides
  - o AAA Tour Book pages

Yellow Pages Advertising
- o Local telephone director

Mailing lists
- o Develop guest loyalty and increase sales by regular mailings
  - o Newsy and informational
  - o Photos of guests

TRUE OR FALSE QUESTIONS
On the following questions, answer whether the statement provided is true or false.

T F 1. Marketing focuses on the needs and wants of guests.

T F 2. Public relations are efforts to make the public favor the restaurant without resorting to paid advertising.

T F 3. Most operators price the more expensive items using the cost-based method.

T F 4. Business plans begin with a market analysis and strategy, which outlines the elements of the plan.

T F 5. The mission of a restaurant is reviewed and changed as often as necessary.

T **F** 6. Price is the only revenue-generating variable in the marketing mix.

T **F** 7. Sales focus on the needs and wants of the guests.

T F 8. Charity affairs attended by the affluent are occasions to collect addresses.

T F 9. Advertising is purchased in newspapers, radio, TV, or similar businesses.

T F 10. The sales mentality exists when the seller thinks only of her or his needs.

T F 11. Under the law, all businesses are operated as proprietorships, partnerships, or corporations.

T F 12. A partnership is legally defined under the Uniform Partnership Act as any venture where two or more persons endeavor to make a profit.

T F 13. A corporation is a legal entity similar to a person in that it can borrow, buy, conduct business, and must pay state and federal taxes on profits.

T F 14. Corporation owners can be sued for the debts of the corporation that they don't personally guarantee.

FILL IN THE BLANKS: KEY TERM REVIEW

On the following questions, fill in the blank with the most appropriate key term.

1. Restaurateurs are placing greater emphasis on _____, the design used to create a special atmosphere.

2. Before embarking on the complex task of setting up any business, especially a restaurant, it is essential to do a(n) _____, which will help increase the probability of success for the restaurant.

3. _____ include deciding who is going to do what and by when and in what order for the organization to reach its strategic goals.

4. Once the target market is identified, it is important to _____ the restaurant to stand out from the competition, and to focus on advertising and promotional messages to guests.

5. Restaurant product can be described as having three_____: the core product, the formal product, and the augmented product.

6. The number of guests at individual restaurants is called the _____.

7. Restaurants, like all businesses, go through _____ from introduction to decline; the trick is to extend the stages.

8. _____ implies determining who will patronize a restaurant and what they want in it—its design, atmosphere, menu, and service.

9. _____ conveys to the customer the best face or image of the restaurant, what people like most about it, or how it stands out from the competition.

10. A(n) _____ is used to show how a restaurant compares to the competition.

11. A(n)_____, is a simple framework for generating strategic alternatives from a situational analysis.

12. The _____, that is the total of all actual and potential guests, is generally _____ into groups of buyers with similar characteristics.

13. Food and labor costs, when added together, are known as _____.

14. _____ covers the quality, pricing, and service of the product offered.

15. Restaurant marketing is based on a(n) _____, which patterns the way management and owners have decided to relate to guests, employees, purveyors, and the general public.

16. The objective of a pricing policy is to find a balance between guests' perceptions of _____ and a reasonable contribution to profit.

17. The _____ may include goals, strategies, tactics, who's responsible, measurable outcomes (metrics), and methods for tracking progress.

18. The average number of guests who would, if all other things were equal, eat at any of the competing restaurants is known as the _____.

19. The _____ analyzes the marketplace, the competition, and the strengths and weaknesses of the existing or proposed restaurant.

20. Doing a(n) _____ will help you to determine the strengths and weaknesses of your restaurant compared to the competition. _____ have one or several co-owners, with only a general partner or partners making decisions, who are legally responsible if things go wrong.

21. _____ have one or several co-owners, with only a general partner or partners making decisions, who are legally responsible if things go wrong.

22. A federal district court judge ruled that an employee that is required to wear what would be considered a revealing and provocative uniform has the right to pursue a case based on the _____.

23. Individual ownerships of a business are called _____.

24. Keogh and _____ plans are both examples of retirement plans that can save a considerable amount of money for an individual.

25. _____ partnerships share limited liability with no services performed.

MULTIPLE CHOICE QUESTIONS: CONCEPT REVIEW

On the following questions, circle the choice that best answers the question.

1. Which of the following is finding out what guests want and providing it at a fair price that leaves a reasonable profit?
   a. Positioning
   b. Segmenting
   c. Sales
   d. Marketing

2. According to the text, the total of all actual and potential guests is called the _____.
   a. buyers
   b. pool
   c. market
   d. target

3. The "S" in SWOT analysis stands for _____.
   a. strengths
   b. segmenting
   c. stresses
   d. sales

4. Which of the following are the three typical market segmentations?
   a. Geographic, Demographic, Behavior
   b. Demographic, Behavior, Style
   c. Concept, Geographic, Demographic
   d. Behavior, Concept, Geographic

5. The only revenue-generating variable in the marketing mix is _____.
   a. place
   b. potential
   c. positioning
   d. price

6. Which of the following conveys to the customer the best face or image of the restaurant, what people like most about it, or how it stands out from the competition?
   a. Differentiation
   b. Positioning
   c. Place
   d. Product Life Cycle

7. According to the product levels described in the text, the _____ product is the function part of the product for the customer.
   a. core
   b. formal
   c. augmented
   d. informal

8. When analyzing the competition it makes sense to do a _____, which shows how your restaurant compares to the competition.
   a. market segmentation
   b. reality benefit analysis
   c. guest potential matrix
   d. comparison benefit matrix

9. The conventional-wisdom method of pricing, which calculates the cost of the ingredients and multiplies it by a factor of three, to obtain a food cost percentage of 33, is called _____ pricing.
   a. cost-based
   b. competitive
   c. forecast
   d. operational

10. When combined, prime costs should not go above _____ of sales.
    a. 20%
    b. 40%
    c. 50%
    d. 60%

11. _____ is like a "mini blog"—it's a series of posts limited to only 140 characters—perfect for any busy restaurateur, bar manager, or chef.
    a. YouTube
    b. Twitter
    c. MySpace
    d. Facebook

12. A part of marketing that focuses on the needs of the seller is called _____.
    a. assessment
    b. sales
    c. demand
    d. analysis

13. The key to positioning is how _____ perceive the restaurant.
    a. employees
    b. guests
    c. competitors
    d. surveyors

14. Demographics include:
    a. age, sex, family life cycle, income, and occupation, education, religion, and race
    b. country, state/province, county, city, and neighborhood
    c. occasions, benefits sought, user status, and usage rates
    d. loyalty status and buyer readiness

15. A _____ analyzes the community, the potential guests, and the competition.
    a. demographic assessment
    b. topographical survey
    c. behavioral survey
    d. market assessment

16. The "W" in SWOT analysis stands for _____.
    a. when
    b. where
    c. weaknesses
    d. wishes

17. According to the product levels described in the text, the _____ product is the tangible part of the product and it includes the physical aspects of the restaurant and its décor.
    a. core
    b. formal
    c. augmented
    d. informal

18. The "O" in SWOT analysis stands for _____.
    a. outside
    b. opportunities
    c. order
    d. offers

19. According to the product levels described in the text, the _____ product includes services, such as automatic acceptance of certain credit cards, valet parking, and table reservation service.
    a. core
    b. formal
    c. augmented
    d. informal

20. The "T" in SWOT analysis stands for _____.
    a. time
    b. threats
    c. top
    d. trends

14. In setting up a corporation, the entrepreneur must keep in mind that to maintain control, he or she must own _____ of the stock.
    a. 50%
    b. 51%
    c. 55%
    d. 60%

15. The simplest business entity, for tax purposes is the _____.
    a. sole proprietorship
    b. limited liability corporation
    c. partnerships
    d. corporation

SHORT ANSWER QUESTIONS

1. Name three benefits of creating a business plan.

2. What are the differences between sales and marketing?

3. What information will be gained from completing a marketing assessment?

4. Name the three most common areas of market segmentation?

5. What are the four Ps of the marketing mix?

INTERNET EXERCISE

1. Search the Internet for restaurant licensing requirements in your area. Make a list of required licenses to share with the class.

ACTIVITY

1. Gather into groups of three of four and brainstorm for ideas of how to market your new restaurant to potential investors. Next, brainstorm for ideas on how to market the restaurant to potential guests.

CHAPTER 15:
FINANCING AND LEASING

INTRODUCTION

Each step in the process of the restaurant evolution, from concept to operation, is important. Finance and leasing are of equal importance to the overall success of the restaurant. The amount of capital required, how much to keep in reserve for the first few months of operation, where the capital is obtained, and how much it will cost to borrow the money are all critical issues. Soliciting a Small Business Administration loan is a lengthy and complex process. Other sources of loans are discussed. Leases are also a complex commitment. Generally leases are for a fixed dollar amount per square foot per month plus a percentage of gross sales, depending on the negotiated terms of the lease. With triple net leases, the restaurant operator assumes the burden of upkeep, taxes, and insurance on the building.

OBJECTIVES

After reading and studying this chapter, you should be able to:
- o Forecast restaurant sales.
- o Prepare an income statement and a financial budget.
- o Identify requirements for obtaining a loan in order to start a restaurant.
- o Discuss the strengths and weaknesses of the various types of loans available to restaurant operators.
- o List questions and the types of changes a lessee should consider before signing a lease.
- o Discuss the strengths and weaknesses of the various types of loans available to restaurant operators.
- o Describe the various forms of business ownership
- o Recognize the legal aspects of doing business
- o Discuss the various types of government regulations.

CHAPTER OUTLINE

Financing
- o Where does the money come from?
  - o Borrowing on property
  - o Relatives, friends
  - o Partnership
  - o Groups of investors

Sufficient Capital
- o Many try to start restaurants with only a few thousand dollars in capital

- o Such ventures usually fail
- o Number-one factor of failure
  - o Lack of management
- o Second factor of failure
  - o Lack of finance and working capital
- o Commercial banks
  - o Common source of funds
  - o Lending officers in the banks
  - o Bank also wants collateral
- o Types of loans
  - o Term loan
  - o Intermediate loans
  - o Single-use real estate loans

Preparing for the Loan Application
- o Restaurateur bought furniture and fixtures from an existing restaurant for $30,000
  - o Money is paid to previous person leasing the property
  - o Paid after a due diligence
  - o Larger restaurants will naturally cost more
- o Important financial questions
  - o How much money do you have?
  - o How much money will you need to get the restaurant up and running?
  - o How much money will it take to stay in business?

Budgeting
- o Purpose: "do the numbers"
  - o Forecast if the restaurant will be viable
- o Sales
  - o Must cover all costs
  - o Must allow for reasonable profit
- o Financial lenders
  - o Require budget forecasts as a part of the overall business plan
- o Basic categories to project sales and operational costs
  - o Sales
  - o Cost of sales
  - o Gross profit
  - o Budgeted costs
  - o Labor costs
  - o Operating costs
  - o Fixed costs

Forecasting Sales
- o At best, calculated guesswork
  - o Many factors beyond control of the restaurant
- o Without a fairly accurate forecast of sales
  - o Impossible to predict success or failure
- o Sales volume components

- o Average guest check
- o Guest counts
- o Once weekly, monthly and yearly sales figures estimated, cost of sales determined.

Income Statement
- o Provides information about financial performance over a given time period
  - o Allows for analysis and comparison of sales and costs
  - o Shows income after expenses have been deducted (net income or loss)

Budgeting Costs
- o Cost categories
  - o Fixed costs
  - o Variable costs

Gross Profit
- o Money left from sales
  - o After subtracting cost of sales
- o Must provide for all other operating costs
  - o Plus leave enough for a satisfactory profit

Controllable Expenses
- o Expenses that can be changed in the short term
  - o Variable costs
  - o Salaries and wages
  - o Benefits
  - o Direct operating expenses
  - o Heat, light, and power
  - o Administration
  - o General repairs and maintenance
  - o Payroll

Uniform System of Accounts for Restaurants
- o Benefits
  - o Outlines uniform classifications and presentations of operating results
  - o Allows for easier comparisons to foodservice industry statistics
  - o Provides a turnkey accounting system
  - o Is a time-tested system

Balance Sheet
- o Used to determine a sole proprietor's or company's worth
  - o Lists all assets and liabilities
- o Must always balance
  - o Assets = Liabilities + Net Worth
- o Snapshot of financial standing at a given moment in time
  - o Usually at the end of a financial period or fiscal year

PreOpening Expenses
- o Include
    - o Initial purchase of all equipment
    - o Hiring and training of personnel
    - o Preopening advertising

Fixed costs
- o If restaurant building is owned
    - o Depreciation
    - o Insurance
    - o Property taxes
    - o Debt service
- o Variable costs
    - o Change in direct proportion to the level of sales

Cash Flow Budgeting
- o Any business needs available cash.
    - o Managing cash is crucial during first few month of operation.
    - o Positive cash flow is enhanced by increasing sales or decreasing costs while maintaining sales.
    - o Can be achieved by: Cash receipts journal, cash flow budget collecting asap

Productivity Analysis and Cost Control
- o Various measures of productivity have been developed
    - o Meals produced per employee per day
    - o Meals produced per employee per hour
    - o Guests served per wait person per shift
    - o Labor costs per meal based on sales
- o Simplest employee productivity measure
    - o Sales generated per employee per year

Seat Turnover
- o Number of times a seat turns over in an hour
    - o Some consider the most critical number
- o Goal rates vary
    - o Seven an hour to less than one an hour

Securing a Loan
- o Only people who are independently wealthy can ignore funding. Everyone else will need to secure a loan.

Compare interest rates
- o One percent over a period of years is big money
- o Avoid points if possible
- o Beware of bankers who demand
    - o Compensating balance
    - o Interest discounted in advance

Loan Sources
- o Include
    - o Local banks
    - o Local savings and loan associations
    - o Friends, relatives, silent partners and syndicates
    - o Limited partnerships

Small Business Administration
- o User-friendly
- o Excellent record of success in lending money to restaurants
- o Principal parties
    - o SBA
    - o Small business borrower
    - o Private lender: central role
- o SBA loan requirements
    - o Right type of business
    - o Clear idea of which loan program is best for you
    - o Knowing how to fill out the application properly
    - o Willingness to provide detailed financial and market data required

SBICs
- o Small Business Investment Companies
    - o Licensed by the SBA
    - o Independently owned and managed
    - o Set up to provide debt and equity capital to small businesses
- o Minorities Enterprise SBICs
    - o Specialize in loans to minority-owned firms
    - o Amounts loaned range from $20,000 to $1 million or more

Soliciting an SBA Loan
- o Qualifications
    - o Be of good character
    - o Show ability to operate a business
    - o Enough capital to operate on a sound financial basis
    - o Show proposed loan is of sound value or secured as reasonably to assure repayment
    - o Show past earnings and future prospects
    - o Provide sufficient funds to withstand possible losses

Sequence for Securing an SBA Loan
- o Items
    - o Current business balance sheet
    - o Income statements
    - o Current personal financial statement

- o List of collateral to be offered
- o Statement noting total amount of financing and specific purpose of the loan
- o Tax returns for the most recent three years

Stockpiling Credit
- o To make the process smoother, provide
  - o Personal financial statement
  - o If in business: History, balance sheet, P&L, cash flow statement, tax statement, etc.
- o SBA business plan required as part of loan application. Seven written sections:
  - o Cover letter
  - o Business summary with name, location, menu, target market, competition analysis and goals
  - o Market analysis
  - o Market strategy
  - o Management plan with organization chart, job descriptions and resumes
  - o Financial data history and financial projections for three years.

Other Sources of Money
- o Include
  - o Landlord or landlord's bank
  - o Local government
  - o Selling and leasing back
  - o Public
  - o Selling bonds or convertible bonds
  - o Farmer's Home Administration
  - o Economic Development Administration (EDA)
  - o Urban Development Action Grant program (UDAG)

Collateral
- o Collateral is security for the lender
  - o Personal property or other possessions assigned as a pledge of debt repayment
- o Most important collateral is character. How does lender determine character?
  - o Personal observation
  - o By references
  - o By credit reputation
- o Collateral accepted by banks
  - o Real estate
  - o Stocks, bonds
  - o Chattel mortgages
  - o Life insurance
  - o Assignment of lease
  - o Savings accounts
  - o Endorsers, co-makers, and guarantors

Keeping the Loan Line Open
- One loan may lead to another.
  - Development of a line of credit is a valuable asset

Avoiding Personal Liability
- Shrewd individual who guarantees a sizeable loan has very few personal assets that can be claimed in case of default.
- Giving one's assets to another may be hazardous.

Leasing
- Restaurant buildings and equipment are more likely to be leased by the beginner
  - Less capital is required
- Signer is obligated to pay for the entire lease period
  - Lease should be good for both parties
  - Beginners should try for a five year lease with an option to renew

Lease Costs
- Approximate five to eight percent of sales
  - Can go as high as 12%
- Lease costs
  - Calculated on a square-foot basis
- Lease terminology and length
  - Consult a lawyer versed in real estate terminology to avoid misunderstandings

Drawing up a Lease
- Ask questions before agreeing on a lease:
  - Why is building for rent?
  - Who was the last tenant?

Lease Terminology and Length
- Both parties should consult a lawyer versed in real estate terminology to avoid misunderstandings.
  - Triple net lease
  - Renewable lease
  - Five- year term plus three five- year renewal options.
- If the business does not survive you are still liable for the payment if you signed a personal guarantee.

Specifics of Most Restaurant Leases
- Annual rent for lease space is calculated per square foot per month and is known as the base rate.

Term of Lease
- Most foodservice leases are for five years with two more five-year options

Power supply
- o Typical retail spaces are provided with 200 amps of electrical service
  - o Negotiate with landlord for cost of repair to site and to run lines from the main panel to the tenant space.

Financial responsibility
- o Who will pay off lease in case, for any reason, the restaurant must close its doors?

Preserve the roof warranty
- o Restaurant owner can either pay the landlord or decrease the tenant improvement allowance

Maintenance agreement
- o Who is responsible for repairs to the building?

Real estate taxes
- o Each city and county decides on the value of land and buildings.
  - o These taxes are typically due once a year, but most ask taxes to be prorated and paid monthly.

Municipal approval
- o Cover your bases by insisting, in writing, that this lease is void if city or county does not approve the location to operate.

Leasing and insurance
- o Tenant is responsible for obtaining insurance against fire, flooding, and other natural disasters as well as general liability.

Restaurant Insurance
- o Types
  - o Property/building
  - o General liability
  - o Business income
  - o Workers' compensation and employers' liability
  - o Employee benefit liability
  - o Liquor liability
  - o Equipment breakdown
  - o Food contamination/spoilage
  - o Crime
  - o Auto/valet liability
  - o Umbrella/excess liability
  - o Fire
  - o Several others

What is Restaurant Worth?
- o Potential Values
  - o Real estate value
  - o Value as a profit generator

TRUE OR FALSE QUESTIONS
On the following questions, answer whether the statement provided is true or false.

T   F   1. Commercial banks take more risks than other lending facilities because they have the largest pool of money to draw from.

T   F   2. Due diligence is a thorough check to assure that everything works and that the health department is not about to shut the place down for some infringement of their regulations.

T   F   3. Fixed costs change proportionately according to sales.

T   F   4. The rapid-turnover style of restaurant generally has a high check average, but produce a low sales volume.

T   F   5. Controllable expense is the term used to describe the expenses that cannot be changed in the short term.

T   F   6. Commercial banks are common sources of funds that people go to when opening a new restaurant.

T   F   7. Variable costs are normally unaffected by changes in sales volume—that is, they do not change significantly with changes in business performance.

T   F   8. The purpose of budgeting is to "do the numbers" and, more accurately, forecast if the restaurant will be viable.

T   F   9. In order to obtain a bank loan you will often need to prove that you have the funds to pay mortgage insurance, taxes, the required down payment, and closing costs.

T   F   10. Lack of finance and working capital is a close second to lack of management when it comes to reasons for restaurant failure.

FILL IN THE BLANKS: KEY TERM REVIEW
On the following questions, fill in the blank with the most appropriate key term.

1.   The borrower should not wait to request a loan until just before it is needed. They should begin to _____ as soon as possible.

2.   Few people entering the restaurant business have the total _____ necessary to enter as a complete owner, debt free.

3.   A clumsy or slow waitperson is a(n) _____ in an operation that depends on turnover for sales volume.

4. _____ specializes in loans to minority-owned firms.

5. Restaurant buildings and equipment are more likely to be _____ by the beginner because less capital is required.

6. When the banker requires a certain amount to remain in the bank at all times this is called a(n) _____.

7. The _____ organization is made up of successful retired business people who work on a volunteer basis to help businesses with specific problems.

8. _____ are independently owned and managed companies set up to provide debt and equity capital to small businesses.

9. When operators or would-be restaurateurs have a choice of lenders, they should, by all means, compare _____.

10. Forms of _____ are the assets that the bank can take should the loan not be repaid.

MULTIPLE CHOICE QUESTIONS: CONCEPT REVIEW
On the following questions, circle the choice that best answers the question.

1. According to the text, sales forecasting for a restaurant is _____.
   a. calculated guesswork
   b. exact science
   c. calculated science
   d. unnecessary

2. The number-one factor in restaurant failure is said to be lack of _____.
   a. promotion
   b. capital
   c. management
   d. employees

3. Costs that are normally unaffected by changes in sales volume are called _____.
   a. variable
   b. uncontrolled
   c. fixed
   d. adjustable

4. There is a _____ success rate of the SBA loans to restaurants.
   a. 25%
   b. 55%
   c. 45%
   d. 65%

5. Which of the following is not a source of collateral for a bank mentioned in the text?
   a. Real estate
   b. Savings accounts
   c. Life insurance
   d. Automobiles

6. Loans cannot be made at more than _____ interest over the prime lending rate.
   a. 2.25%
   b. 2.50%
   c. 2.75%
   d. 3.00%

7. Single-use real estate loans typically run less than _____ years.
   a. 20
   b. 25
   c. 30
   d. 55

8. A term loan is one repaid in installments, usually over a period longer than _____ year(s).
   a. 1
   b. 5
   c. 10
   d. 15

9. A standby amount of cash to open the restaurant and to get through possibly several unprofitable months of operation is called _____.
   a. capital
   b. profit
   c. collateral
   d. income

10. Expenses that can be changed in the short term are called _____.
    a. uncontrollable
    b. controllable
    c. fixed
    d. compensating

11. The banker requires a certain amount to remain in the bank at all times. This is called having a(n) _____.
    a. retreating discount
    b. advanced discount
    c. compensating balance
    d. assessment balance

12. Costs that change proportionately according to sales are called _____.
    a. variable
    b. controlled
    c. fixed
    d. unadjustable

13. Intermediate loans are made for up to _____ years.
    a. 20
    b. 15
    c. 10
    d. 5

14. Banks want assets that they can take if a loan is not repaid, this is called _____.
    a. swindling
    b. collateral
    c. negotiating
    d. capital

15. Which of the following best describes lending officers when it comes to loans?
    a. They maximize risks.
    b. They are largely judge on the amount of loans they approve.
    c. They tend to be ultraconservative.
    d. They tend to be negligent.

16. A construction loan is made in segments during the course of construction and is usually a(n) _____ loan.
    a. intermediate
    b. term
    c. single-use real estate
    d. adjustable

17. Ordinarily, unless the individual has established a line of credit, the bank wants at least _____ (and usually more) of the total needs to be invested by the individual or corporation.
    a. 20%
    b. 30%
    c. 40%
    d. 50%

18. The purpose of the _____ is to provide information to management and ownership about the financial performance (profitability) of the restaurant over a given period of time.
    a. income statement
    b. balance sheet
    c. productivity analysis
    d. budget forecast

19. Sales minus _____ equals gross profit is a standard accounting entry.
    a. cost of sales
    b. labor costs
    c. operating expenses
    d. sales volume

20. The _____ is used to determine a sole proprietor's or company's worth by listing all the assets and liabilities.
    a. income statement
    b. balance sheet
    c. productivity analysis
    d. budget forecast

SHORT ANSWER QUESTIONS

1. A restaurant has two potential values: its real estate value and its value as a profit generator. Explain the difference between the two.

2. A hypothetical restaurant is a space of 8,000 square feet leased at $8 per square foot. What would the monthly rent would be?

3. What would the annual rent for the above restaurant be?

4. Why are restaurant buildings and equipment more likely to be leased than purchased by the beginner?

INTERNET EXERCISE

1. Search the Internet for buildings available for restaurant leasing in the ideal loc␣ ␣on of your choice. Be sure to note the leasing costs. Next, search your local area. H␣ ␣ do the locations differ in regards to costs and square footage?

ACTIVITY

1. Create a diagram of your choice illustrating controllable and fixe␣ expenses for a restaurant.

CPSIA information can be obtained at www.ICGtesting.com
Printed in the USA
BVOW04n0430190814

363070BV00002B/3/P